"WHO TOLD YOU YOU WERE NAKED?"

The counterfeit compassion of culture.

THOM HUNTER

Thom Hunter's books can be ordered through booksellers or by contacting:

Thom Hunter
Thom@Bridgebackministries.com
authorthomhunter@yahoo.com

ISBN-13: 978-1466493322
ISBN-10: 1466493321

And the God of all grace, who called you to His eternal glory in Christ, after you have suffered a little while, will Himself restore you and make you strong, firm and steadfast.

1 Peter 5:10

THANK YOU --------------

Thank you to the encouraging people in my life who share words of love and support and who understand forgiveness and grace . . . or at the least yearn for that understanding. I appreciate the vision imparted to me by people who have learned to speak truth and show compassion, wavering in neither. Some of you I know well; others I may never know in person, but, because of what you have shared with me, I know you as a brother or sister. We walk together.

Through it all -- and "all" is a much bigger word than it appears -- my wife, Lisa, has been so filled with grace, so loving, so hopeful, so encouraging, so sure of God's overwhelming presence, that I owe her more than any mere dedication can reflect. Still, I dedicate this book to Lisa because she loves truth and bestows grace and, in spite of me . . . loves me still, as I do her.

CONTENTS

GRACE

INTRODUCTION

"Where is God? ...Go to Him when your need is desperate, when all other help is vain, and what do you find? A door slammed in your face, and a sound of bolting and double-bolting on the inside. After that, silence." – C.S. Lewis, after the death of his wife.

God is omni-present; but it seems every now and then He is omni-absent. The sign on the door says "Gone Fishing," the lights are out, the doorbell dings in an empty room, the No Vacancy sign is on . . . drive on down the road . . . alone. Yes, I know that is not true; He never leaves me; He never leaves you. He's right there.

How can Someone as magnificent as God be there . . . and we be so unaware?

Wasn't He there, in the Garden of Eden, right *after* Adam and Eve's encounter with the serpent? His Word says God came walking up in the cool of the day. Surely He was also there in the heat of the moment. Yet He didn't clear his throat and wag his finger and say "Ummm . . . Eve . . no, no, no." So Eve did, did, did and we've been done for since.

God was oddly silent as the sin unfolded and then clearly loud as the consequences unraveled the beautiful original intentions of existence.

I'll admit that it bothers me a bit to know that God is with us before we slip into the comfort zone of our sinful nature and, with all the power of the universe at His disposal, watches us tumble, twist and turn on the way down, and hit the bottom with a gut-wrenching and bone-jarring thud. Then comes out in the cool of the day as if He had not seen it all happen. Is He really a "what's up?" God?

No.

"Wait for the Lord. Be strong and let your heart take courage. Yes, wait for the Lord." -- Psalm 27:14

But we don't want to wait. We want to act. We want to meet a . . . need? We *want!*

How many of us, when we are dialing a number we shouldn't know; turning into an area we shouldn't go, logging on to a website we shouldn't see, acting like someone we shouldn't be . . . say to ourselves: "Wait . . . Let me ask God about this?"

It's easy to say He's not speaking when we're not pausing. It's pure spiritual finger-pointing to say He's not responding when we're not reflecting.

I think sometimes we think we might prefer a "No . . . No . . . No . . ." wagging-a-warning finger God. And we would of course gently lay down our pride, sweep aside our defiance, thank Him profusely for keeping us from falling, pledge our undying trust and obey without question. Or perhaps we would eat of the fruit; gain the knowledge we do not need; satisfy the glutton side of our spirit and waddle into our all-too-familiar rescue me mode.

Fact of the matter is, God does wag a "No . . . No . . . No . . . "finger in our faces. We just ignore it and say we didn't hear Him. Are we actually expecting God to sit by our bedside and read His Word aloud to us at night?

My son, do not forget My teaching, but keep My commands in your heart, for they will prolong your life many years and bring you prosperity. Let love and faithfulness never leave you; bind them around your neck, write them on the tablet of your heart. Then you will win favor and a good name in the sight of God and man. Trust in the Lord with all your heart and lean not on your own understanding; in all your ways acknowledge Him, and He will make your paths straight. Do not be wise in your own eyes; fear the Lord and shun evil. -- Proverbs 3:1-7

OK . . . we'll do that. But . . . remind us. Okay, God? We just might forget.

Oops . . . that was how the verse began: "do not forget." And it asks us to "keep." Keep what? Those commands we so easily tossed to lighten the load as we traveled down the me-want road. And . . . oh yeah . . . He wanted us to write "love and faithfulness" on the tablets of our hearts. But . . . that's *my* heart. There's not much writing room left; I've done a lot of scribbling and mark-outs through the years trying to satisfy the longings of my heart.

Of course then He wants us to trust. Trust the Creator or lust for the creation? Tough choices we face in this life. He says if we trust Him instead of ourselves . . . He will take all those crooked detours, jagged fault lines, dangerous drop-offs, and impossible mountains . . . those cliffs . . . out of our paths and make them "straight." We're not talking sexual semantics here . . . we're talking direction . . . which certainly *can* lead to some serious sexual semantics.

So what else does this "silent" God, who watches us one once again slam a door in haste, have to say? He says for us not to be wise in our own eyes. Who knew that the pursuit of wisdom could be so dangerous? Well . . . Eve, I guess, in retrospect. Adam, too. And, oh yes, the serpent. They all learned it, but God knew it all along. Surely God doesn't want us to just be stupid? We'd get into so much trouble. Oh . . . yeah. That.

For the foolishness of God is wiser than man's wisdom, and the weakness of God is stronger than man's strength. -- I Corinthians 1:25

I remember driving out onto a lonely hill at the edge of the town I grew up in, seeing the lights in the distance and thinking of each of them as a porch light in a home where everything was right and good, every body tucked in for the night, every heart satisfied, every mind at rest, every soul at peace.

Lacking the courage to call out to God, I repeated instead within my mind what all was not right with my world . . . my home . . . my heart . . . my soul . . . my peace. And those words echoed within the emptiness . . . and brought me heartache. I had come to the hill alone . . . and remained there alone . . . and departed alone. *My* choice.

We may come to the garden alone . . . but we shouldn't leave that way. He is so accessible, but He might want us to linger a little longer than we want. So, we dash and slam. "Oops . . . sorry."

What must really be difficult for God -- if anything could ever be so labeled -- is to hear the echoes of His own Word as it descends into our valleys and reverberates against the emptiness we feel as we seek to satisfy our selves with increasing self-absorption. We want to move that mountain, cross that valley, swim that ocean . . . and then . . . when totally satiated, cry out "Where were you, God?"

With you.

I know sometimes it *seems* we are all alone in whatever battle has worked to separate us from His love, whatever temptation has tattered our goodness, whatever sin has led to our shunning. But we are never alone. We would not, could not, will not be alone.

Having trouble finding your own way out of your mess? Tempted to blame God, declaring Him absorbed in some sort of Solitaire while you slowly slip away?

Maybe we would hear more . . . if we would open a few doors here and there instead of slamming them as we proceed to and fro on our own. Maybe if we played a little less hide-and-seek, put away a few must-see and must-have distractions -- the pursuit of happiness as defined by culture -- and paused at the table, talked to Him, listened to Him, pulled out the chair, sat down . . . and waited.

Like He asked us to do in the first place. Remember:

"Wait for the Lord. Be strong and let your heart take courage. Yes, wait for the Lord." -- Psalm 27:14

You know, that's what I always wanted: to be strong, to have courage. And He said I could. If I would wait for Him.

Next time you find yourself feeling the pain of self-induced pity at your pitiful plight of weakness in the face of temptation, remember: Wait. Be strong. Take courage.

Wait.

We don't do that very well, do we? Waiting. Waiting on the Lord. In the face of a nagging want . . . we choose not to wait for Him to speak first. We don't ask; we proceed, usually with little caution. We follow the lead of a swallow-up, smother-down culture which promises enlightenment and satisfaction, leaving us later to stumble, dazed and damaged, into the light to face the daunting question: "Who told you you were naked?"

Choosing to follow is a day-to-day decision which can lead us to victory or defeat, restoration or repetition, onto a straight path or into an endless cycle.

God is never silent. He spoke it all, in advance of every question.

.

TRUTH

CHAPTER 1

PERMISSION NOT TO LISTEN

All we ever need to know in life we can learn on the treadmill with our earphones on.

Not really.

But . . . I have learned some things in the afternoons on the treadmill at the gym, switching channels to distract myself, grazing between talk shows like *Dr. Phil* and, a while back, *Glenn Beck* and *Oprah Winfrey* . . . with a little *That '70s Show* and *Jeopardy* spliced in during commercial breaks. The collective, subjective, highly-suspect and often conflicting wisdom delivered by those in search of ratings and reactions could tie a brain in knots and split a heart into a million pieces and send the soul on an endless search for satisfaction. Or, we can make sexual confusion a clever punch line and laugh it off entirely. So many opinions to weigh and people to please. We may not always be a captive audience, but we're a certainly thirsty one, taking full advantage of the technology and the glitz . . . and the messages of the hosts and guests, all carefully edited and sharpened to a point.

To make their point. They don't know you; they don't know what you are going through; they won't be around if you do or don't make it; they just want to shine a little junk-life light . . . and move on to the next titillating or sorrowful subject. Tears all around; hankies in abundance.

Cut! It's a wrap.

Generally what you learn from the talkies is that glitz and guts count more than truth and glory when it comes to deciding what

Why do we seek other voices when He said "listen?"

Why do we rush from door-to-door when He said His would open if we would but knock?

Why do we run toward cliffs of uncertainty when He said "come" . . . "now" to the calmness of certainty, the satisfaction of settling?

We're filling the void with the wrong voices pushing the wrong choices. We can read . . . we can hear . . . we can speak . . . we can share. We could care . . . if we'd dare.

And we need to exercise the discipline of discernment and give ourselves permission not to listen. Don't become a disciple of mis-direction.

Dare to love and look for those who do. For real. Not like Ricky on a sound stage, or Elton behind diamond-studded glasses, or Ellen dancing around in tennis shoes laughing, or Neal Patrick Harris in a sitcom, or Oprah in adoration-fueled self-celebration. True love is not rated by a Nielsen meter. True love is measured by the heart-wrenching moments that lay the stones for a safe crossing from where we find ourselves to where we long to be . . . and where we long to not arrive alone.

Love like Christ, giving, longing, seeking, teaching, healing, helping, seeing, hearing, saying, changing. LOVING. Truth, not glitz. Giving, not taking. He forgives us for what we became and He changes us to what we should be. He comes alongside so we don't have to wonder where we're headed. He guides us forward, over and around the obstacles, not hiding them, but conquering them. He doesn't erect new roadblocks along a route of rejection.

Their talents and riches aside, these actors and singers are just people like the rest of us, tempted in a fallen world. I would never wish them harm -- indeed I wish them wholeness -- but I do wish them truth, so they could use their voices to lead other strugglers to freedom instead of only to ticket lines and concert halls. Blind guides.

In a world frightfully flinging itself along to no-where, Jesus proves the patience of love and says "Come." "Now." He is always ready, always waiting.

And the Help of the helpless says . . . help others.

The third time he said to him, "Simon son of John, do you love Me?"
Peter was hurt because Jesus asked him the third time, "Do you love
Me?" He said, "Lord, You know all things; You know that I love you."
Jesus said, "Feed My sheep." -- John 21:17

Did I hear that right? If I love Jesus, I will feed his sheep? But, hey . . . what about me? I'm hungry too . . . but it's when I forget to turn to You.

When we turn to anything other than Christ, we find ourselves surrounded by the plentifulness of it all, but starving from the emptiness. Unfortunately, we often disguise that emptiness with the wagging of our tongues and the proclamation that all is well and getting weller by the day. That's another time people need permission not to listen and the ability to see that the truth is not in you.

If I speak in the tongues of men or of angels, but do not have love, I am
only a resounding gong or a clanging cymbal. -- I Corinthians 13:1

Christians are out of tune on the truth about sexual and relational brokenness, gonging and clanging, offering headaches for heartaches . . . and the mute button is getting a workout. We often don't know religious from righteous, Christianity from churchianity; hope from a hole-in-the-ground, mercy from meanness, forgiveness from forget it, love from leave. We teach restoration, redemption and rescue. And then we run from the reaching.

"But do not have love?" There's the rub. All those polished words we preach are but the cymbals from which the clanging erupts. We're not real in voice or deed. We memorize the verses and know the applications, but not enough of us really love. Yes, some do . . . but the church is a collective, a body. Believers require too little of each other, even as we demand a great deal from the broken who would love . . .love? . . . to join us and share in what we say we have, if they could trust in the truth of it. Peace. Mercy. Grace. Wholeness. More often, we have a detailed list, tuned to their repentance and we follow-through on it with an eagle eye.

I'm not lamenting the lack of love demonstrated toward me when I was hiding in the church like a broken boat towed into harbor, weighted with guilt from an out-of-control obsession with a love-me temptation that had twisted itself into a use-me fixation. I understand the need for true confession and real repentance, the need for them to know for sure I was actually a sheep . . . and not in wolf's clothing. Actually, the lack of love I experienced fuels my need to share it so clearly now. A calling from the falling. In its own way, that vacuum was a blessing.

Do we love Christ? Then why are the sheep so hungry? Will they find what we withhold somewhere else out there in the welcoming wilderness among the wolves who . . . want them . . . in ways Jesus never intended for His sheep to be devoured in their weaknesses?

If someone comes to the pantry door, weak and thin, hand outstretched, not feigning faintness, but near to falling, we fill their cup. The sexually-broken are no different. They are weak, fading, fearing, losing feeling, so-often falling they might not know which way is up . . . fill the cup. Don't sound the gong. Don't send them to drink from the stagnant creek of a cackling culture instead of the living water of an endless river of grace.

Jesus bore the debt and bore the burden, yet too many Christians can barely bear the sight. If the sin of others repulses you in a way that your sins don't, pray for forgiveness for your lack of forbearance and God will give you strength.

If you yourself are among the homosexual, the pornography-addicted, the adulterer, the lust-bound, then keep your courage and keep coming. In the body of the church are the hands and feet of the faithful who will love you and walk with you and speak truth into your lives, catching you with compassion when you fall until you finally stand and live beyond the chains. They may be too few, but they are better than the "it gets better" bunch.

There really is a way out, but it takes a double-dare. One dares to seek. Another dares to care. Both dare to love. In the absence of cymbals they hear each other; truth wins a battle and sin slithers away in darkness.

Listen.

Jesus said "Come." The world is watching to see if we agree with Him . . . and not with them.

CHAPTER 2

THE FUTILITY OF AN IF-LESS LIFE

The tempter came to him and said, "If You are the Son of God, tell these stones to become bread." -- Matthew 4:3

I was reminded today how difficult it is for Christians to be Christian. Usually such reminders come by accident, or seeming happenstance, though, as a Christian, I have to accept the fact that today's unsought, unwanted, unappreciated but unavoidable meeting with one of the church leaders from a mystifying moment in my past might have been purposeful, as in God-ordained. Taco to taco.

That's so . . . God.

I have been "blessed?" to witness the worst and the best of Christian behavior, ranging from the wrap-around of real extended grace to the messy and misguided attempts by Christians to go all-out WWJD, most often with people who could care less what Jesus would do because their lives are crying out for *us* to do something. When we respond from behind our Christian masks instead of risking our Christian skins, our blessings are scorned by the rejecting responses of those we quickly label as rebellious and on ruinous routes to hell. We can easily find that our "you" is showing and our "me" is rising to the surface, as in WWID, major emphasis on the "I." We don't see the hurt in the other's eyes because of the great pain we ourselves are feeling when our efforts are disdained by those who don't trust or revere us. Believe me . . . I've seen this from both points of view.

We Christians are all, after all, only people, washed and clean but heading smack-dab back into the ever-alluring mud of life. We may forever hope to avoid that slippery slope, but it seems to be a fixed point on many a personal compass. Like moths brought to light or dogs to a fight, we flit about and find ourselves burned or bitten. Indeed, the ever-present inner flaw that leads us into repeated desperate situations is one of the best arguments against evolution. If we were evolving, surely we would do better by now.

We try to summon common sense, but common sense is not much of a savior. Good sense is not really that dependable and certainly not that common. So we find ourselves in and out of situations, depending on our skills at manipulation, even before we realize how God might have intended them to unfold.

That's so . . . human.

When I look back at some of my most drastic falls from grace -- as we humans might characterize them -- I realize that I was always falling *into* grace, not out of it. Still, no matter how healing the landing might eventually become . . . the fall gets the attention, as we ricochet against the treacherous walls of whatever abyss we have been dancing along the edge of. Looking up from the hard and cold and dark and enveloping bottom of our pit of choice, we ask "why?" In other words, God, if You really love me, why don't You stop me?

Better yet, we want to know why what we do has to be constituted as a fall in the first place. Could not God have created a constant plane and set us upon it to travel throughout a life that cannot trip us up? Why all these bumps, these curves, these hills and valleys, these disturbing and deceitful detours? If You really are God . . .

That's so . . . shall we say . . . Satan?

If we did not fall, would we ever call? If we did not slip, would we ever grip?

And there's the rub: that little word "if."

If we *would* just call, might we not fall? If we *would* just grip, might we not slip?

If only. Then perhaps those drastic "falls from grace," would never take place.

For instance, what if in those desperately-seeking-someone days of discovering adulthood I had thought of my Christian friend as a brother and not as a potential source for satisfaction? What if I had seen him as God sees him and not as I wanted to see him? What if I had been to him what God wanted me to be instead of being a me that just wanted? If the if had turned a different way would I have avoided decades of distancing acts that often made God seem but just a shadow? I think I see clearly how those bumps and valleys we call tests and trials emerge onto the paths on which He lays out His plans for us.

What if we open this door . . . instead of that one?

What if we listen to this person . . . instead of that one?

What if we close our eyes and ears and refuse to see or listen to God at all?

What if we choose to stray instead of pray?

What if we hide the Word somewhere far removed from our hearts?

What if we give up and give in instead of giving ourselves to Him?

What if we refuse truth because it confuses the world-skewed view we have learned to accept of ourselves?

What if we demand of God and then use His response to justify our rebellion because He does not turn our sought-out stones of life into pillows to give us rest?

What if we judge Him by the actions of His people?

What if we pile onto Him all the pain and all the rejection and all the confusion and all the delusion and all the wandering and all the wondering and all the sorrow and all the loneliness and all the fear and all the hate and all the emptiness and all the deceit and all the craving and all the lies and all the arrogance and all the judgment and all the shame and all the guilt and all the hopelessness?

Really . . . what if we did that? What if we just said to God: "Take that!"

He would.

He will. It's not a matter of if.

If I was 25 or 35 or maybe even 75 and had never struggled with sexual brokenness, this is the place in this story where I would tell you to just give it all to Him and you won't have to

11

struggle anymore. And you could slap your palm against your forehead and say "duh" and get on with your life. But, as a Christian who struggled and fell so often that down seemed up, I won't do that to you. I know how it feels to be lectured by plank-bearers who cannot see you through the cloud of disdain that replaces grace with grey.

But I will tell you this. The Bible is not joking when it tells us to take up our cross daily and follow Him. That doesn't mean bear the burden; it means die to self and surrender to Him. Every day. It's not a miracle cure; it's a daily dose.

Actually, when Jesus said it, He began with . . . "if."

"If anyone wishes to come after Me, he must deny himself, and take up his cross and follow Me. For whoever wishes to save his life will lose it, but whoever loses his life for My sake and the gospel's will save it.
-- Mark 8:34-35

That's an if we can all live with . . . and an if we cannot live without.

Okay . . . back to the taco. We made a little small talk, asked a few tentative questions, perhaps made a little progress? Perhaps. Perhaps we turned a few stones into bread . . . or burritos.

CHAPTER 3

WHY BE BOTHERED BY THE TRUTH?

"We just want to offer a positive message that being gay is not something you have to apologize for. It's simply one of the great and diverse ways that God has created us. Being gay is a gift from God."

-- *Dan Rutt, Central United Methodist Church, Toledo, Ohio*

Our local Cane's Chicken is my favorite place to hit and grab a quick meal on a busy Saturday when I'm not in the mood to make decisions of delectability.

"Three-finger combo please."

The sign says chicken, the menu says chicken, the box contains chicken. Yes, you can have fries with that, but not much else; maybe some delicious buttery bread and an ice cold drink . . . with a little too much ice. Eat, enjoy, toss and get on with the to-do-list. Cane's allows a little leeway for those who believe cole slaw makes a suitable non-fried side, but . . . basically . . . it's all about the chicken.

I like that. Sometimes I just want to know that there really is a real meaning for the word "is." I like to sit down, get comfortable, open the box and say, this is chicken.

Truth in a booth.

I'm confused, which is a problem when it comes to the truth, as to why we are becoming so dissatisfied with the truth. Are we just bored? Are we so enamored with ourselves personally that we have to one-up God somehow and reinterpret the "The Way, The Truth and the Life," by removing each "the" and replacing it with a "my?"

My way? My truth? My life?

If there is no real hell, and if being gay is just another gift from God -- which God apparently forgot to list with the other ones in the Bible, by the way -- then why should we be troubled with the truth at all?

Truth? You show me yours and I'll show you mine. Hell seems so old-fashioned in the light of enlightened culture. Blessed affirmation of inner gayness may tickle some ears that shy away from divine grace and Biblical truth, but people's lives are more important that a popularity contest.

And that's the truth.

In light of all the purveyors of deceit -- by intention or ignorance -- it might be a good time to remind everyone that discernment really is a gift from God.

Perhaps we could settle all this gay stuff right now by just marking off 50 paces between the Westboro Baptist Church-cult people ("God Hates Fags") and the Central United Methodist Church-misled people ("Being Gay is a Gift.") and let them fight it out. Wouldn't that settle it?

I doubt it. A truth for a truth?

So, with all this swirling around us, it seems the perfect time for a reminder that it is okay that we *sometimes* doubt and wonder, but unless we turn to the God of Wonders, we *always* will.

One of the hardest things anyone with a significant struggle -- such as same-sex attraction, pornography addiction, heterosexual lust or any addictive temptation -- deals with, is doubt. Self-doubt, sure. But, also the doubt others have in his or her ability to change . . . or even doubt that the person really wants to change. Sometimes this doubt is not truly expressed, but is instead hidden behind the "we're with you" smiles, which can so quickly become "we knew it" frowns at the very first sign of a fall. How nice it would be for all involved if this battle were but a minor skirmish with a certain outcome, instead of one of those "well, I had my doubts all along" battlefields, littered with the wounded, some doubting they can get themselves back up again to move forward, some doubting if anyone even cares anymore.

I had a friend in college who lived with no doubts. He was always sure his project would be the best. He would sing the song just fine. His parents would, of course, send the money. His car would run. His jokes would always be funny and people would laugh. He would always be understood. His friends would ever be loyal and everything would complete itself perfectly, right on time. He was never timid or understated because he never doubted. But, he was also pretty much tied up in secret knots of frustration. He'd exchanged doubt for denial. When he *didn't* win first place or his joke fell flat or the check didn't arrive or the tire went flat or a friend let him down, he would bottle up inside and close down. What most of us might have lived through as dashed hope he died to as devastation. His forced-open eyes would fill with tears of anguish. He definitely needed some doubt.

I haven't seen him in many years, but I "doubt" he is as certain of everything as he used to be.

Some might say my friend had faith. But the presence of faith is not the absence of doubt anymore than the presence of doubt is the absence of faith. Faith is based on a belief in hope. It involves assurance . . . and trust. This friend lived on assumption, not assurance. A little too much "it'll be all right," and a little too little "what will be will be." He had no faith to test because he allowed no doubt.

But what if we have a lot of doubt? Does that mean we have little faith?

I remember I used to sit on the curb in front of our house on Saturdays when I was a little boy. I doubted my dad would show, but I had faith that he would. Could the measure of each -- doubt or faith -- be determined by how long I sat with my chin on my knees looking to the left and right to see if he might come walking up the street?

I have no doubt God clearly knows the difference between doubt and faith. I'm not sure we always do. On our own, we usually reward our doubt with our deepest fears. Our faith, on the other hand, is usually God-tested and leads us to our greatest joy. "A little while" of testing can feel like a long time . . . and produce an awful lot of doubt.

15

In this you greatly rejoice, though now for a little while you may have had to suffer grief in all kinds of trials. These have come so that your faith -- of greater worth than gold, which perishes even though refined by fire -- may be proved genuine and may result in praise, glory and honor when Jesus Christ is revealed. – I Peter 1:6-7

It used to bother me that, of all the Biblical characters, I was named Thomas. The doubter. I know my mother did not really name me Thomas because she was debating which Biblical character I would be like. After all, my brother's name is Mike, and my sisters' names are Deb and Sue. Mother was merely reflecting the popular name choices of the decade in which we were born. We could have as easily been Bob and Gary and Judy and Peggy. But I was Thomas, the doubter.

I think God loves those who doubt. In dealing with our sincere doubt, He demonstrates the truth that He is patient and kind. It is a wonderful truth that the greatest doubters often become the greatest believers. Our honest doubts can become the bedrock of our faith. Truth that comes rampaging in to dispel doubt is sweet and strong.

Maybe we should think less about what doubt is . . . and less about who doubts us . . . and instead think about what doubt may do. How does it motivate us? Does our doubt send us searching or hiding? Revealing or masking?

Doubt is like looking out the window and seeing the sun go down for the gazillionth time, knowing once again that the darkness will follow, mimicking the darkness inside us. We might forget momentarily that the sun is only gone for a while. It does not yield its place to darkness in God's creative balance. Through grace, the light comes back around to overwhelm the darkness . . . lest anyone doubt. We strive hard to resist letting our sexual sin define us; let's not let our doubt do it either. You've read the Bible. Yes, people wander, but they are never beyond the gaze of God.

But what of those who doubt us or the sincerity of our quest for freedom? I say, let each doubter bear his own. Sometimes we expend so much energy trying to dispel the doubts of others that we have too little energy left to put on the armor for our own battles. Let them doubt. God can deal with that. And, if

16

they want someday to put their hands in your scars, scarcely believing this new you is . . . you . . . then let them do so and forgive their doubt as you forgive your own.

Some may tell us we've used up all our chances. They've moved beyond doubting to knowing. "You can't change." Well . . . life is not a game of chance; it is a reality of faith. Let them keep their assumption; you have your assurance.

I am thankful for doubt. Anyone who struggles with temptation knows that doubt is a glimpse of freedom. If we can doubt, we can seek.

Doubt leads us to the door. That door where you knock. Where you ask. That door that opens. Behind which no despair lingers. Where doubt no longer dwells.

"Ask and it will be given to you; seek and you will find; knock and the door will be opened to you. For everyone who asks receives; he who seeks finds; and to him who knocks, the door will be opened."
-- Matthew 7: 7-8

And if for some unfounded reason you doubt that the word "everyone" includes you, let that doubt lead you to the door. It will open . . . no doubt.

CHAPTER 4

DENIAL REALLY IS A RIVER

The view from the banks doesn't tell us how deep
Is the beautiful river that flows.
As the babbling sound of the water that speeds
Calls out to our landlocked souls.

We hold fast on the shore, skipping rocks in the swells
As the sun's light repaints the deep blue
And the water moves on carrying with it the hope
Of a life we so want to renew.

A life spent on dry land, with a river in sight
A life thirsty and wanting for more
We keep longingly searching as day fades to night
And the river's voice grows to a roar.

We will know where it goes when we take the first step
Leaving shoes in the mud at the side
Into the beautiful river that flows clean and clear
And is endlessly deep and wide.

    I've never been very good at self-introduction, perhaps because it always requires a little panic-stricken introspection, a super-fast sorting, a quick evaluation and a rapid response. From kindergarten on, we're always being asked to tell the world -- or at least a little crumble of it -- a "bit" about ourselves in those quickly-forgotten "we really do want to know you" moments.

"Tell us in a nutshell who you are . . . just a little bit about you," he says with a smile. Or she says with a grin. Then silence . . . waiting . . . waiting . . . looking around the room; people gesturing encouragement.

"Just a few words," she says. "A couple. Please?"

And then, in a nervous burst of energy, we answer and it's done. Can we please move on to the next person in the group?

"Well, I like to play football, watch science fiction, read novels, cook, sky-dive, sketch architectural designs on napkins, re-build engines and I enjoy landscaping in my leisure time. Oh . . . and I memorize Scripture. 'Jesus wept.'"

Polite applause and on to the next person in the circle.

With a brief sigh of relief, I always knew that my limited self-revelation would be accepted. Probing rarely went beyond questions like, "well, if you were a tree, what tree would you be?" I was responsive, but rueful, supplying the right answers to the wrong request: "Tell us in a *nutshell* who you are." Thank goodness the request was not for a boatload.

"Well, I struggle with unwanted same-sex attraction and I'm always a little worried that maybe that will never change and my world will collapse around me because I'm not being who God wants me to be and I'm concerned about the whole smiting thing . . . and people finding out . . . and being hated . . . and rejected . . . and humiliated . . . and . . . "

Oops. Boatload.

For Christians who battle a relentless and unwelcome sexual temptation, walking the fine line between who we really are and who we want others to think we are, puts us in constant danger of falling out of the boat and into the river. Some days we would welcome being swept away to a peaceful place downstream. Most days we tread water and fight currents. We know that "what you don't know" *will* hurt you and it will hurt me, so we don't tell. The facts become so deeply buried that leaving them there could hardly be called denial. Right?

Then He called the crowd to Him along with His disciples and said: "Whoever wants to be My disciple must deny themselves and take up their cross and follow Me." -- Mark 8:34

There are a lot of important words in that verse:

He *called* -- Jesus wanted to make sure everyone heard Him. He didn't whisper; He called.

The *crowd* -- Jesus was telling everyone they had an opportunity, not just a few people here and there.

Whoever *wants* -- So, yes, He was talking to everyone, but it was only going to work for the ones who wanted it.

My disciple -- Not someone else's or something else's.

Deny -- Hmmm . . . there's a requirement here.

Themselves -- Now that's interesting. Not some dark deed or a Hostess Twinkie, but self? Each one?

Take Up -- Action words again. Mercy . . . first you have to listen . . . then you have to want . . . then you have to deny . . . and now you have to take up? Take up what? And where is this leading?

Their cross -- Oh, that. You take yours; I'll take mine.

Follow Me -- Wow, easier sung than done. "Where He leads me, I will follow." Drat those distractions.

Ummm . . . Jesus? Would You mind if maybe I take up someone else's cross and follow you? Would that work? Perhaps the skydiver guy's? Mine is too heavy and someone might see me dragging it around. Actually, someone might trip and fall into the deep furrows behind me.

I'm not only not unfamiliar with denial, I'm practiced at it. Unfortunately, though it was clearly denial, it was the *wrong* kind of denial, the hiding behind a self-projected and self-protected self, instead of a laying down of a self-rejected self. As you can clearly see, I was a bit full of . . . my self. That's what the wrong kind of denial does. It spins us into a spiral of sorting and picking, piecing together the parts of ourselves we want to display, practicing comfortable answers to discomforting questions. It can lead to a deadly dance of the despairing Ds: deny, deceive, delay, depart, decay, destroy. Depressing.

I don't think Jesus is asking us to come screaming out of our shadowy recesses and declare our dastardly deeds and caustic compulsions and twisted temptations and startling stumblings like some leper calling out before himself a warning to all who hear. Sometimes transparency is better accepted by those around us after a bit of healing has taken place . . . after a season of cross-bearing and following Him. In a perfect world, Christians would be able to bear *their own* crosses and lend *you* a hand with yours, but most can't and few will. I've discovered some of those few and am amazed, but realize they do so only through Christ. Unfortunately, we live in that imperfect world where even Christians feign shock at sin, perhaps having only glanced at the pages of God's Word, creating a simplified view from selective verses.

We sin. We fall. We plunge headlong into Satan's schemes. And the cross gets all the heavier it seems as we get all the weaker. And then, just about the time our face is about to hit the rocks, we hear . . .

"Come to Me, all you who are weary and burdened, and I will give you rest." -- Matthew 11:28

Don't you just get so tired sometimes that you want to throw your hands up and say, "I give up. This is me. Get over it." You want to proclaim yourself free from the struggle, refusing any longer to deny "who you really are?"

That's not denial. That's acceptance. That's not soaring into freedom; it's settling for bondage. It really is giving up, not giving up our selves. Perhaps the denial of denying is one of the toughest temptations of all, leading to a disastrous surrender. "I just can't." Who wants to go thump-thump-thumping down a long and hard road stooped over with a cross on his back when it is so much easier to just log on to a computer and let your eyes glaze over at airbrushed pictures or meet up with another wanderer trying to convince himself he's used up all his tokens for the turnaround turnpike and may as well see where the dead-end ends?

You're right. You can't. That's the thing about denial. When you deny yourself, you become His. Remember? That was in the verse too. That was the promise. "My disciple." Jesus loves His disciples. You think He won't be looking over His shoulder as you fall in behind Him bearing your cross? You think He's going to let you slide down into the dust with a "too bad, so sad," retort because your cross was too heavy in the early-going?

If Jesus didn't love me . . . if He hadn't forgiven me . . . if He didn't want me . . . if He didn't need me . . . I'd chuck this cross into the mighty river, have a picnic and watch it fade from view into the horizon. But He does . . . and I won't.

Yes, it's hard. And you will have to bear the ignorance of those who think your sin is worse than theirs and that you are less than they. That's just a cross you'll have to bear.

But you don't have to do it alone.

CHAPTER 5

Chutes and Ladders: Extreme Edition

"I don't want to play anymore."

I remember when my grandchildren used to come to the house. In warmer weather they wanted to be outside to pick the garden of still-green fruit or pluck the flowers or maybe just pick up rocks. Wandering around the yard like little ducks, stopping here and there to point and stare at wondrous things so often overlooked by the rest of us on our way to somewhere. Little ones are just . . . there. Where they are is the somewhere that matters.

On colder days, my grandchildren would dash down the hall and head for the toy room, a place that still held the baby bed in which all five of our children had slept and in which some of our grandchildren had risen from their own naps to stand and point at games and dolls and briefly-wanted things beyond their reach. Help was always on the way.

"Anyone want to play?"

And, if not answered quickly enough and affirmatively enough?

"Play with me."

And two little hands would hold a box and look above it to gauge the expression of the bigger one who is being roped in and will soon sit creaked and cross-legged on the floor and unfold the board and place the plastic markers to begin the game. With patience, toss the dice and move the player pieces when they reach a point on the board too distant for the little arms to reach.

Put them back in place when a tiny sneaker kicks and skews the game, sending pieces flying. Set it right again and go on.

Patience. Someone will win. Or someone will get hungry. Or distracted. Or called away.

My grandson loved the *idea* of chutes and ladders -- climbing and sliding -- but he also was pretty clued in on winning. When he learned that the chutes (slides) would take him back where he'd been, he would try to skip them and head for the next ladder, falling back on the can't-count-good excuse that sometimes works for children. Enforce the rules and a few chutes more . . . and you see a little face slowly turn serious.

"I don't want to play anymore."

A lot of times, no one won "Chutes and Ladders." There were always other games to play. Or cookies.

Who can blame him for wanting to win? When you think about it, embracing the ladders, the hard climb up, should make you a winner. Who puts those dumb chutes in the way, sending us sliding back down, starring at empty spaces . . . and more ladders? Life gets tiring and the finish line -- the victory -- seems to just slide away, so close and yet so far.

During the long, long struggle to find victory over sexual addictions -- unwanted same-sex attraction, pornography, lust, idolatry -- we long for ladders that will take us up and out to higher places and clearer views. Who puts those dumb chutes in the way?

Two steps off the ladder and your skimming down the loneliness slide. "Where did everyone go?" becomes "where is someone?" *Anyone?* And there you are, searching and seeking, not where the ladders lead, but in the pits at the base of the slide where what looks like love and feels like love will do for love for now. Yippee . . . the wind from the wild slide blowing through your hair as you glide into the mud at the base. Well . . . that was fun, as they say, for a season.

Crawl to a ladder. Hold on, rung by rung, eyes straight ahead, resisting the impulse to slip over to the slide nearby and go for another ride. Remember . . . those things only go down.

I rarely see God as a grandfatherly being. I have always pictured him as benevolent, willing to reward richly those who try and those who cry and those who need and those who want and those who seek and those who speak . . . to Him. He's the master of the ladder. "Know my son? Take a rung."

As I did with my grandson, God occasionally just has to enforce the rules. You roll the dice and there you are standing at the edge of a chute and God says . . . go. There will be a ladder down there when you land, and if you get up and climb again, you will eventually finish this . . . game? It's not a game at all. It's just the way. And it does take a will. Conformed to His.

What really often happens is we decide -- from weariness or loneliness or hopelessness -- we can just change the rules . . . and all those ladder-detractors say Amen.

Life gets easier under the new rules. The mud gets cushy and familiar. We want chutes of grace and slides of glory, but no ladders of righteousness or steps of repentance. Before long, we forget to even look up. Who knew there was a way out of here? Who wants to leave anyway? This is culture at its coolest. After all, aren't we supposed to love each other?

It's very dark at the base of the chutes and before long the light at the top of the ladder looks like the farthest star. How cozy. How choking.

Climb.

You can do this. Keep your eyes focused on that distant light which comes closer with each rung you put behind you. Ignore -- it's not cruel to do so -- the calls of culture coming from those who want to re-write your journey as they slide by you on the chutes, hip-hollering and smiling all the way down, trying to make you feel dumb for all your exertion.

You've heard all the arguments and they really do have it wrong, no matter how self-revealed they may be. Some of them know, deep inside, that they're wrong, and are prolonging the inevitable climb from the mud. Others may never know . . . unless perhaps we who scale the last rung, call down, lean over and extend the hand that makes the climb more likely for others.

Focus and you will find that God does not ever lead us into meandering. Every step along His path is progress. He even told us how to stay on course. *THINK.*

Finally, brothers and sisters, whatever is true, whatever is noble, whatever is right, whatever is pure, whatever is lovely, whatever is admirable -- if anything is excellent or praiseworthy -- think about such things. -- Philippians 4:8

> Focus on whatever is true. (Step on the ladder.)
> Focus on whatever is noble. (Take another rung.)
> Focus on whatever is right. (And another.)
> Focus on whatever is pure. (And another.)
> Focus on whatever is lovely. (And another.)
> Focus on whatever is admirable. (And another.)
> Focus on on whatever is excellent. (And another.)
> Focus on whatever is praiseworthy. (You're there.)

Think. When you find yourself in the deepest pit of sexual out-of-controlness, or listening to the voices that try to convince you you are on an impossible chase en route to an inevitable self-acceptance that collides with every description of God's desire for you, what are you thinking? Of the truth . . . or in desperate search for a palatable lie? Of something noble . . . or something passable? Of something really right . . . or something someone just tells you is? Of something pure . . . or putrid? Something lovely . . . or something self-satisfying? Something admirable . . . or some place to hide? Something excellent . . . or something barely mediocre? Something praiseworthy . . . or something that separates you from the One worthy of praise?

So kick the board with your sneakers and send the pieces flailing and get that serious look on your face and look up from your cross-legged position on the floor.

Just tell God . . . "I don't want to play anymore."

Maybe it's finally time to leave the toy room behind and go outside.

CHAPTER 6

THE BOGEYMAN MYTH OF THE HATEFUL BIGOT

Jesus said, "Father, forgive them, for they do not know what they are doing." And they divided up his clothes by casting lots. -- Luke 23:34

I have been told the church was mostly silent. Evidence of my ongoing struggle with homosexuality was presented, a vote was taken and I was declared unfit to be a member and removed for the destruction of my soul. I was not there that night, but instead was angry and alone in the darkening end of a long and frightening day, as they proclaimed me unworthy of them. Oh . . . my soul. And all that is within me.

I have not seen, in the years since that fateful vote, the faces or heard the voices of those present on that night. No simple note, no gentle whisper of hope or reminder that a prayer has gone forth on my behalf. No Christmas card. No condolences on the burning of my home. Nothing. Separated with only a shred of hope for reconciliation somewhere in eternity.

And yet my soul remains secure. It was not destroyed, but was instead strengthened by the knowing that there is One, who *was* there that night, who is always with me, and who always will be. Who truly knows my soul.

I have re-invented the scene in my mind's eye. Presumed which scriptures were cited. What examples of my betrayal of all-things-Christian given. I knew the pain of my children was displayed to support the need for the harshest penalty possible for

27

my sexual sin. And, like a late-night bogeyman emerging from behind a closet door with sword drawn, eyes glaring and lips pursed, they produced a greater fear than that inside me, a sharper pain than my own self-induced judgment. Shame. Rejection. Aloneness. Unworthiness.

And then, well, life pretty much returned to normal for all of us, each seeking God and each falling short, sometimes knowing what we're doing, but often not. And, as God does, He looked beyond their rejection and my self-revulsion and on to redemption and restoration, accepting my repentance.

I thought of them then as the bullies of the pulpit, bearing down on a witless victim already buried beneath the debris of his bad decisions. "Here . . . we'll make this one for you. You're outa' here."

Hateful bigots?

No.

Bewildered believers?

Yes.

Many times we are unable to separate strugglers from embracers; those who fight and fall under the relentless pull of a never-wanted homosexual attraction, from those who wrap themselves in it in a shrill proclamation and flaunt it in the face of believers, bating a response they can declare as hateful, damaging and destructive babble from an ill-informed hateful bigot. They build a bogeyman and feign fear so the cries can drown out the truth and stifle the motivation of compassion.

It is a useful myth and, in its relentless repetition, it divides us and reduces us to lessening relevance. And some no longer care. We surrender and adopt a code of silence.

How dare we?

Have we forgotten that behind the face of the loud and lost lies a heart that God longs for regardless of whether it longs for Him? Is our only choice to thicken the walls and batten down the hatches? Can we only put on the full armor of God to assume the attack mold? Are we to cover our eyes with the hands which should be reaching?

The pro-gay agenda is making ground with the weapon of two simple words: hateful bigot.

"You don't want me to be happy? *You hateful bigot.*"

"You don't think I should marry my same-sex partner? *You hateful bigot.*"

"You believe in a God that thinks I sin just by being . . . who He made me to be? *You hateful bigot.*"

"You say you love me and then quote your scriptures that condemn me? *You hateful bigot.*"

"You want me to be like you? *You hateful bigot.*"

"You drive me to suicide with your judgment and ignorance and bullying and your chains and you make me feel so unloved and rejected and put down . . . and, on top of that, you deny my civil rights and don't want me to be proud of who I am . . . and you think you're just better than me, that's what. *You hateful bigot.*

Repeated over and over and over, the myth becomes, to some, a twisted reality. And while we will always have hate and we may always have bigots, they are remarkably few among bewildered believers.

And yet, we know that homosexuality *is* a sin and *is* destructive, as all sins are. Sins are indeed "evil" and can pollute the soul of the man to the point he becomes inseparable from the sin . . . outside the prying power of love.

"An evil man is rebellious to the core. He does not fear God, for he is too proud to recognize and give up his sin. The words he speaks are sinful and deceitful; he does not care about doing what is wise and right. He plans ways to sin while he lies in bed; he is committed to a sinful lifestyle; he does not reject what is evil." -- Psalm 36:1-4

Christians who are brave enough to love will find themselves surrounded by men and women who struggle with unwanted same-sex attraction and only want help in the rescue. Their lives hang in the balance. They are the softer targets of the hateful-bigot propaganda machine. If pro-gay advocates can convince the silent strugglers that we -- the bewildered believers -- are anxious to pounce on their revelation with the full wrath of religious fervor, marching to the beat of the resounding gong and the clanging cymbal, the pro-gay advocates claim more casualties and we lose more chances to help heal hurting souls.

We can't afford this. We have no excuses. Even if your upbringing tells you that somehow the homosexual struggler is a lesser human being, a poster-child for "the least of these," then you have a greater responsibility than ever, according to Christ. And, in risking a moment to move into his or her life, you may discover that that shipwrecked soul is destined by God to sail and do great things.

We have no excuse for hatefulness. It comes back to haunt us and diminish the impact we can have in the lives of those for whom hope lies just beneath a clouded surface. We have the truth and if we wield it skillfully, we can tear away the lies without destroying the person who has fallen for them.

What is the easiest way to kill a myth? Live the truth.

"Teacher, which is the greatest commandment in the Law?"
Jesus replied: "'Love the Lord your God with all your heart and with all your soul and with all your mind.' This is the first and greatest commandment. And the second is like it: 'Love your neighbor as yourself.' All the Law and the Prophets hang on these two commandments." -- Matthew 22:36-40

That's the truth. We may not be able to change everyone, but we are not given the choice on whether we will love them. And if we love them, we may well change them, or, at the very least, present a better picture of a God who loves them . . . still.

Don't feed the myth.

CHAPTER 7

How to Survive in the Center of Spin

Speak and act as those who are going to be judged by the law that gives freedom, because judgment without mercy will be shown to anyone who has not been merciful. Mercy triumphs over judgment! -- James 2:12

"Not guilty."

These are two of the most anticipated words of finality ever spoken, returning breath to a room, returning life to a man. At the same time, those two words often do little to erase the pain of those who felt sure they had been wronged, had borne the brunt of another's action, had sought what seemed to be judgment and hear what feels like a two-word announcement of emptiness. For them, breath fades.

Evidence and arguments, claims and presentations, defense and prosecution end with two words, or one. One less word can mean the end of freedom, the weight of penalty, a turning of a key, either in a clanging door of physical separation or in the hearts of those whose hopes rested on hearing the two-word verdict and now begin a soulful separation. Drop the "not," and you are . . . guilty. Said and done.

I've only been a part of two trials in my life, both now years ago. In one, I was on the jury. In the other, I was the defendant. On the jury, I listened and watched as the details of a man's moment of passion was debated and claims were presented. Did he or did he not attack another man, knife in hand? For what purpose? The question for the jury was whether he had exercised justified anger and self-protection, or had sought vengeance and intended serious harm to an undeserving victim.

"Not guilty."

The view as a defendant is seriously different. You hear words designed to deny or justify the truth of the accusations made against you and your spirit lifts because you are sure everyone will understand and extend mercy. Then comes the crushing weight as the prosecution paints you as the scourge of society, leaving you desperately longing for a hole in the floor. Give me the key; I'll lock myself away. One moment I looked like a pity-worthy man who had succumbed to the siren call of sexual temptation and made a fatefully poor decision leading to a regretful conversation followed by handcuffs and dry heaves. The next moment, I resembled more the mass murderer, marching along the edges of society picking off every shred of decency left in the nation, a menacing threat to all that ever was or will be good.

"Not guilty."

Then we all left and went home, pondering mercy. As I said, years ago.

That's how it works in isolated courtrooms with controlled situations and rules and rulings. It may be chaotic at times, but clarity prevails, depending on the presence or lack of "not."

But that's not how it works out here, where we all are, making our own judgments, treating mercy like it is on the verge of extinction, forgiveness as if it is a treasured antiquity to be preserved on a high shelf somewhere, and grace as if its value depends on the tightness of its rationing. Setting aside these commodities, we place the defendants -- sinners -- in the limbo of an ever-hung jury.

Sexual sinners -- in particular those who struggle with and even act out on homosexual temptations or pornography addictions or adulterous lust -- are the centerpiece of this constant cultural contention. Repent or relent? Give-it-up or just give-in? They drive on the yellow-line down the middle of the road of life, dodging the inevitable head-on collisions. It's a constant swerve, with angry fists raised in the passing traffic: "Choose a lane!"

Good advice that.

Swerve into the left lane (not politically-speaking): While driving in this lane, you will be allowed to go as fast as you want, as far as you want, whenever you want, with whomever you want, for as long as you want. It is, of course, the "Whatever you want" lane, paved in affirmation. You may not be sure where you're headed, but no one is going to stop you, so have a nice trip and enjoy yourself. It's all good.

Swerve to the right (again, not politically-speaking): Proceed with extreme caution, observing all signs and speed limits. Keep both hands on the wheel, eyes straight ahead, remove all distractions and keep your license and verification handy for frequent roadside checks, because we are keeping an eye on you. For safety's sake, of course. An occasional equipment check is in order, just to make sure you really are running right.

Let's start with the brakes. Maybe it's time for a rest stop. It seems to me the more enlightened we all become about sexuality, the darker the journey becomes for the sexually-broken. And . . . in an odd twist . . . the two "sides" are becoming more similar in their defenses and prosecutions. Affirmation is becoming a dirty word, used not to affirm you, but what you do. Hence, the hung jury, composed of the muddled masses just wanting to be left alone while someone else sorts it all out, which, of course, God is doing. But does that mean God wants us all just to stay on the courses we've chosen, watching everyone careening along, some in blissful ignorance and others en route to disaster?

Of course not.

If you are a struggler, once you escape the noise of all the traffic around you, you still have the same choice. Do I act on this temptation, or do I not? Either way, why?

The value of asking for directions is diminishing, even though there's no shortage of information and definitely no shortage of *mis*information. Depending on who you ask, the answers range from "you were born this way," and "you have been blessed with the gay gene," to "you're only doing this because you have been led astray and are now seeking your own way," to "God hates you."

Welcome to sexual brokenness in the age of spin.

Sorted out: You were *not* born this way. There is *no* gay gene. You *probably have* been led astray. We *all* -- sexually or not -- tend to seek our own way. And . . . heaven forbid, God does *not* hate you.

While everyone is busy debating, the decision is still up to you. It's time to shut out the silly and go back to the basics. And basically, no matter who is cheering from what sideline, the only voice that can lead you down the right path is still that still small one -- the voice of the One who made you, knows you, loves you, wants you, and will forever keep you if you will just take your hands off the steering wheel and ignore the roadside attractions.

Yes . . . storms will rage. Debate will ensue within and without about what you've done and who you've been and what it all means. Fingers will either curl up to say follow me . . . or point out like daggers to say get thee behind me. You will be declared as either blinded by your own overestimated self-worth or blind to all conviction. The blind will always lead the blind.

And yet . . . there you are. Human, in need of fellowship, hungry for forgiveness, in want of wisdom, hopeful for change, longing to confess, desiring to repent. Roaming from ravaging in sin to rooting among the pigs and crying to come home.

Help? Occasionally, instead of those beckoning fingers and those pointing fingers, you will find a set wrapped around yours, a hand that holds yours and hangs on. A squeeze that frees.

On the road again. But this road beckons us to righteousness. It's curbed with truth, paved with compassion, striped with understanding and laid out with infinite wisdom. It's quiet, as the voices of the ones who either want to figure you out or straighten you out fade away with the sights in the rear-view mirror. If you decide to follow God, you need not concern yourself with the flow of the traffic, and you can pretty much ditch the rear-view mirror altogether.

"*I Have Decided to Follow Jesus*" is an old hymn most of us heard and sang when we were young, We can still recall the tune and words of the five verses that lay out the path-markers that will help you navigate to freedom, regardless of the never-ending debates about your soul and worth and sexual sin, and whether you can ever confess enough, repent enough, or do enough to earn the forgiveness of men.

I have decided to follow Jesus.
Though I may wonder, I still will follow.
Though none go with me, I still will follow.
The world behind me, the cross before me.
No turning back, no turning back!

The confusion of culture in this era of spin and the hopelessness of the ever-hung jury has not changed the rules of the road: Know where you are headed. Don't get distracted. Rest in the Lord and you will make it home. Follow Jesus. No turning back.

Some *will* go with you.

CHAPTER 8

CHRISTIANS AND SEX: THIS IS NO TIME FOR SILENCE

Do not conform any longer to the pattern of this world, but be transformed by the renewing of your mind. Then you will be able to test and approve what God's will is -- His good, pleasing and perfect will. -- Romans 12:2

I always wanted to sing, but never had any confidence in my voice, nor did I ever learn to read music. Still, that didn't discourage me from joining the First Baptist Church youth choir. The summer trips were great; the youth musicals inspiring, the snack suppers worth the effort. The choir sounded great too, but I can take no credit for that. I did not want to be heard, so I kept my voice so low it couldn't have added much,

If I got a little too loud in practice and Mr. Shadle would hear a bass off key, he would silence all the tenors, altos and sopranos and ask the bass guys to sing alone, walking back and forth in front of us, leaning in with a hand cupped over his ear. He never found me; I would just mouth the words as he approached and let the other guys carry the weight for all the sound. I made the choice to have no voice. I didn't contribute much to the singing and, because I was hiding, I never got the instruction Mr. Shadle might have given me, so I really still can't sing on key . . . at least not on purpose.

When it comes to the chorus of sexual chaos into which this current generation is falling, I think a lot of Christians have made the choice to have no voice, opting to let others carry the tune. Many Christians are choosing cowardice over courage;

callousness over compassion; indifference over love; comfort in ignorance over strength in truth.

What are we afraid of?

Headlines paint a picture of a nation obsessed with sex, not in the way of the google-eyed fraternity beer-boys in weekend football commercials, but in a disastrous dead-end way diminishing individuals and dealing death. Indeed, we're beginning to see life basically defined by sexual identity, a dwindling down of self-worth that leads to division and judgment . . . and endless pain. And Christians, if they're not just sitting it out on the sidelines are too often speaking harshly and arrogantly, putting more distance between them and ones who need them. Sadly, some of the most judgmental people in public may not regularly be in church, but they often cite scripture and portray themselves as advocates of righteousness.

So, what is true? The truth is that, scripturally, any sex outside of a marriage covenant between one man and one woman for life is a sin. The truth is that Christ died for all sinners, sexual or otherwise. The truth is that people who are confused about their sexuality and think themselves gay, or people who find themselves addicted, or people who find themselves giving into temptations, having sex with the same sex, lusting after someone other than their spouse, staring at pornography on their computers, fantasizing . . . are people who, like you, were made in the image of Him, and like you -- and all other sheep -- have gone astray.

The truth is, they are as loved by God as you are . . . and the truth is when one of them jumps off a bridge, or leaves a spouse, or hides in a closet, or moves into a dangerous and misdirected lifestyle, we should weep and pray . . . not point and parade in our own over-rated righteousness.

Maybe we're afraid of looking tolerant, so we settle for looking ignorant instead. But . . . *tolerance* does not necessarily mean *agreement*. Being tolerant of others is not a compromise of our own beliefs, it is a demonstration that we know and understand that sin can and will wrap itself around the mind and heart and soul, and only Christ can break those bonds. We're not privileged to know how and when He will do so, so we continue on in hope and love. If we demonstrate our conviction that a relationship with Jesus is the only way to have a relationship with God, then we need to tolerate people we disagree with and be prepared to witness to them . . . and we can do so without endorsing their ideas. If our personal convictions are true and strong, they are not endangered.

When it comes to sex, we don't much teach and we don't much preach. And we certainly don't reach, as in out. While our pews on Sunday have their share of pornography addicts and same-sex strugglers, rare is the church where any effort is made at all to provide a safe place for confession, accountability and repentance. To most of the sexually-broken, church looks more dangerous than a dark corner in a Mafia-run Mexican village. Our message is simple: "Just don't. And if you already do, don't tell us." We have some "don'ts" who will and will never look for help. We have some "already do's" who would die before revealing. And some of them are dying inside within easy reach of the light.

Are we obsessing about sex? Consider these recent events:

Jerry Sandusky, an assistant football coach at Penn State, was accused of recruiting young boys through his charity organization and sexually abusing them.

Bernie Fine, assistant basketball coach at Syracuse University, was fired after allegations he molested boys

Presidential candidate Herman Cain was being dogged by women who claim he sexually-harassed them and by one woman who claimed to have carried on a 13-year adulterous affair with him.

These three men found themselves in the sexual spotlight. Questions about sex and our society are becoming more common, more consistent and more consuming.

A judge declared that "Don't Ask-Don't Tell" should not be enforced in the military, no matter what the military itself or the American people think.

Married Minnesota Vikings quarterback Brett Favre was accused of sending sexual messages and naked photos to a female sports reporter and other women.

Bishop Eddie Long, leader of a 25,000-member megachurch in Atlanta, faced accusations of sexual coercion from four men, former parishioners.

The U.S. Supreme Court considered a free speech case against Westboro Baptist Church, an independent "church" group that protests outside military funerals with signs that say "God Hates Fags."

A judge overturned California's Proposition 8, which banned gay marriage, and Attorney General Jerry Brown declined to appeal, despite the will of the people having already been expressed at the ballot box.

New York Gubernatorial Candidate Carl Paladino was declared homophobic by his opponent for saying that children should not be "brainwashed into thinking that homosexuality is an equally valid and successful option."

Teenagers across the country have committed suicide after being taunted as allegedly gay. One young man in my own hometown of Norman allegedly went home after a public City Council meeting recently where an ordinance to celebrate GLBT month was debated and he shot himself in the head. The remarks made at the meeting were demeaning and callous, with no regard for who might be harmed by the painful condemnation.

Authorities arrested 10 people in the Bronx, N.Y., in connection with the brutal assault of two teens and an adult who police say were tortured for being gay.

Porn filming was put on hold because a major porn "star" was infected with the HIV virus. According to Family Safe Media, a new porn film is shot every 39 minutes in the United States alone, and more than 50% of Christians report that pornography is a significant problem in their homes.

Teen pregnancy and sexually-transmitted disease rates continue to rise. Statistics show that more than 60% of teens have had intercourse before high school graduation.

The U.S. Customs Service reports there are more than 100,000 Internet sites offering child pornography.

Scan the Internet and you will find countless more headlines about sex. And while the bullying of the gay teens has brought that particular issue to the forefront and created a sense of sensitivity, the underlying issue is the fact that the church has ceded sexuality to culture. Christians may not condone what once would have been considered a sexual revolution, but has now become our sexualized reality . . . but we are accomplices in our silence, from the pulpit, in our homes, in our own lives. We're not adequately putting forth an alternative for those who are trying to find their identity through sex. And we're not showing grace to those who have fallen into one of Satan's most attractive traps. We leave them thirsting, we scrimp on forgiveness, we withhold entry on the only path to redemption because, why? We're afraid we'll get tainted? Misunderstood? Labeled as either tolerant or intolerant or as moral bigots? What tender hearts we have become toward ourselves, even as we have hardened our hearts toward others. Surely we cannot be satisfied to let Ellen and Oprah handle this. Let's not assuage our guilty feelings by watching coverage of candlelight vigils for the ones who took their own lives in despair, not when we are called to be the light.

Woe is me is not an expression of faith.

Too many Christians gather together to lament the fact that the world -- somewhere out there -- is going to hell in a hand-basket. We shake our heads back and forth with pained expressions, declaring the sexual perversion of the modern day must be a sign of the end times. For some, sexual brokenness may well usher in their personal end time, as they find themselves drowning in sexual addictions down the street from the sanctuary door. If we really believe the end is near, should we not be working ever harder to take them with us?

Truth Should Trump Tradition

Some Christians have ingrained Leviticus 18:22 so deeply into their spiritual psyches that they cannot find any room to combine it with the slightest vision of love and grace and forgiveness and healing. Dismissing the sexually broken homosexual with a lifted chin and the word abomination, they live in a world dominated by their memories of "Daddy says all homos go to hell" and that settles it. Why can't they reach out to the ones they would so easily condemn and quote from 1 Corinthians?

"And such were some of you. But you were washed, but you were sanctified, but you were justified in the name of the Lord Jesus and by the Spirit of our God." – I Corinthians 6:11

Toss the Winnie the Pooh Routine

There's too much head-scratching "What's a bear to do?" and not enough "I love you." Why do we find it so difficult to love someone who struggles with sex? If we show love, we open doors. If we open doors, we enter lives. If we enter lives, we have a chance to speak the truth of God's grace to heal and restore all of the broken. Why do we determine that some brokenness is beneath us and beyond God? There's too much hand-wringing and too little hand-folding; too much pointing and too little praying. And, when we pray about something, should we not also ask God what He might want us to do about it? As in "do."

Quit Hiding behind the Smokescreen of Indoctrination

We so often point fingers at the media, the entertainment industry, educators, liberal lawmakers, college campuses and say they are indoctrinating our youth. Why are our youth not already indoctrinated with the doctrines of our beliefs? Why are they so easily taken down in cultural challenges? We make jokes about having "the talk" with our children and yet, by the time some parents get around to it, the child has moved beyond the talk . . . to the touch.

We are too silent.

We have forgotten that a life lived well is a demonstration stronger than any indoctrination. We have forgotten that personal demonstration day-to-day has greater influence than parades on Pride Day. We have forgotten that we are to love our neighbor. We have forgotten that it is that very love by which we are to be identified.

If we are Christians and we are not hurting for others because of what we see, then we have allowed the influence of

41

culture to make us indifferent. If we are hurting, and we are doing nothing, we have allowed culture to make us impotent.

How much longer will we pretend to be a mighty choir, but only mouth the words?

It may be that your church is an exception to the rule when it comes to providing a biblical, truthful and compassionate response to the sexually-broken. If that is so, I hope you will leave a comment below to serve as an encouragement for other Christians to step forward and stand with no rocks in their hands, as Christ would.

What programs does your church have in place to help the sexually-broken? Who in your church has been trained to counsel the boy or girl, man or woman, who struggles with homosexual temptation to help them find support? What are the materials and where is the support for the porn-addicted Christians in your church? What is your church's position on restoring an adulterer? Who will you go to at your church for counseling if your son or daughter says "I'm gay?" And, are you ready if your brother in Christ comes to you and says he is struggling with sexual addiction and needs your help?

Wait. Is that silence?

CHAPTER 9

THE MOUSE THAT KEEPS ON ROARING

I confess to having been a sinner my entire life, revealed by my own actions, always in danger of being smashed like a gnat by someone big enough to demand retribution . . . but always in hope of being picked up and set free again by someone big enough to forgive.

I've often perched on the top of a magnificent peak, foreboding with the potential for destruction, but dazzling with its view of hoped-for restoration. Better there, though, than down in the valley where those who refuse to acknowledge their own worldly shortcomings mingle with those who don't believe they can ever be forgiven and lifted out of the chilly shadows of darker days. All of their energy goes into trying really hard not to bump into each other in the limited space such ignorance allows, so they slowly drift into motionlessness.

I would rather need rest from the drain of repeated bouts of attempting to conquer than from the weariness of aimless wandering.

When I was about 10, I remember walking into the living room where my stepfather had fallen asleep with a cigarette in his hand, his limp wrist a few inches from the amber-colored ashtray on the end table. Ashes had already fallen onto the table and onto the carpet, both of which bore burn marks from past days of dangerous dozing. I took the cigarette from his hand and placed it in the tray and he didn't so much as move a finger or release a grunt. Perhaps I saved an apartment building, or even a life. His perhaps.

That was a good thing.

Before I turned away, I noticed his wallet sitting on the table. Contemplating the alcohol-aided deepness of his breathing, I saw an opportunity. With the insight of a pre-teen sinner, I plucked the wallet from the table, took a few steps away and sifted through it. Mainly one-dollar bills, but plenty of them, and some bigger bills too. I took only what I needed for the moment, knowing he would never notice, or if he did, he would only wonder if perhaps he had stopped at the corner bar on the way home and had one more drink than he could remember.

So, I stole a few bucks, hopped on the bike, headed to the U-Totem a few blocks away and bought an ICEE for myself and a friend.

That was not a good thing.

I've never confessed that before. I've justified it, of course. He was mean and stingy, self-absorbed and really bad at parenting. He never understood me. He was extremely sporadic with weekly allowances. He always had money for a shot of whiskey but never for an ICEE. And I think he just didn't like me very much. So . . . there you go. I couldn't help it. It was all "he's" fault.

Really, the only justification now that seems even slightly acceptable is that I was simply 10, wishing I had a normal dad and a normal life and a pocket full of change to share with friends who would never ask where it came from. I saw a temptation that could be fulfilled easily and with little chance of discovery due to the ignorance of the one being perpetrated, one who was fast asleep while the world moved on around him.

Gay culture is like the 10-year-old who perceives he has not much, but has easy access to a whole lot and will take full advantage of the ignorance of those who sleep, robbing them blind as they drop their ashes on the floor in silent slumber. Gay culture glides into the room, leaves the wallet of life as we know it a little bit lighter and we think we did it to ourselves somehow. Which is, in a sense, the truth.

And gay culture's list is endless as they point fingers of justification at the less-enlightened: *They* don't really understand us. *They* are so mean and stingy. *They* don't want us to be happy. *They* are ignorant, Bible-toting scaremongers. *They* are homophobic. *They* are behind the times, rebelling against reality. *They* like power and want to keep us down. Bless their little-bitty backward souls, *they* just don't know no better.

I've been writing about "sexual brokenness" for years now, focusing on the sin nature that causes many of us to stray from what God intended for us sexually, finding ourselves lusting for same-sex encounters, or transfixed in pornographic fantasy, or lusting after a co-worker or "friend" into full-blown adultery. I've also focused on the truth that God can restore us and put us on paths to righteousness. With His help -- and way-too-often with His help only -- we can maneuver that path, ignoring the spring-loaded temptations that pop up like wildflowers in the median, preening to be plucked if you dare to dash through the lanes of oncoming traffic.

The righteousness of the redeemed should be roaring like a mighty waterfall and the echoes of the healed should be reverberating in our churches and our homes, celebrated as proof that God does indeed love us all, each and every one, never gives up, holds us in the palm of His hand and gives truth to all the words we sing and pray.

That would be good.

But the little pipsqueak roar of the mouse that is gay culture is drowning us out while the ignorant sleeping church just finds a more comfortable position in the worn and cozy recliner. Most Christians wont take the time to arm themselves with the truth of scripture. nor acquaint themselves with the truth of culture. So, we snooze while the world as we know it reshapes itself to quiet the mouse.

A recent study by the National Center for Health Statistics and the Center for Disease Control and Prevention shows that only about 1.4% of the U.S. population actually consider themselves homosexual. Another study from UCLA put the figure at about 1.7%. Though it's a small number, we know and believe as Christians that there is not one soul unworthy of Christ's death on the cross. God bless the 1.4.

The issue is not whether to love those who identify themselves as gay. We should, just as much as we love our own

45

grandmother who probably conforms a little more closely in our minds to what we think God created His people to be. But, loving someone does not mean we conform to their world, which is what is happening.

Christians are way too much like the cowardly lion whose courage vanishes in the presence of a louder voice. We've become the "let's just not go there," bunch. Pretty soon, we won't have much choice . . . or actually, we'll have to make a lot of choices to remain untouched by the cultural backwash.

Instead of fortifying our faith, we're fortifying our walls.

Instead of seeing the homosexual as one of God's children who needs to hear the truth in a compassionate way, we turn all shrill and say "they're after our children" and we turn away.

Instead of seeing the homosexual as one who needs to be beside us, we mutter beneath our breath, "get thee behind me."

And then we turn on the TV and watch young women lip lock after singing songs of broken love. And we turn on a legal drama and find ourselves observing lady lawyers discussing legal options while sharing a pillow. We re-define marriage, re-manufacture the military, re-shape anti-bullying to focus on sexual identity, re-phrase references to avoid bring re-painted as intolerant, refrain from sharing the truth because if we keep our thoughts to ourselves we can avoid being regarded as uncool. We cower in the shadow of the mouse.

Homosexuality is not the real enemy here. It is sexual brokenness, rising out of empty or abandoned relationships, broken homes, unprotected children, disregarded vows, weak wills, ever-better-presented temptations. The apple is even more polished now than when it was in the perfect garden and we are frenzied in our efforts to take a bite.

In his craftiness, Satan has made homosexuality both a jewel and a demon. Those who embrace it will give their lives for it. Those who bedevil it will spend their lives running from it.

And those who are broken -- not gay, but so wanting for a good relationship with someone of the same sex or so fearful of one with the opposite -- move closer to disaster while we marvel at the decibel level of the mighty mouse that keeps on roaring. And our daughters pose provocatively, seduced by emptiness and longing, while our sons invest their souls in pornography like a temporary sedative for an unsatisfied and distorted desire. And our marriages fail as we fall into others' beds.

As I wrote in *Surviving Sexual Brokenness: What Grace Can Do:* "Honestly . . . would it hurt that bad for us to just be honest with each other? Sexual brokenness -- whether it manifests itself as homosexuality, sexual addiction, pornography, idolatry, adultery, self-satisfaction through masturbation or another form -- hurts. It wreaks havoc. It can destroy the broken one and devastate the lives of those who are close enough to feel the impact of the personal implosion. In the meantime, while we debate whether it is too painful to be truthful, we let culture administer so much anesthetic that all affected become numb."

If we take our naps and leave our treasures unguarded, we will lose our hearts as well. Without our hearts, we fail to love. And without love, we fail at everything. The mouse's roar cannot be drowned out by a clanging cymbal.

Gay culture is a mighty mouse . . . and it has not come to save the day.

Wake up.

CHAPTER 10

THE LENGTHENING SHADOW OF PRO-GAY THEOLOGY

For the time will come when people will not put up with sound doctrine. Instead, to suit their own desires, they will gather around them a great number of teachers to say what their itching ears want to hear. They will turn their ears away from the truth and turn aside to myths.
-- I Timothy 4:3-4

SPOILER ALERT:

Pro-gay theology is untrue.

I remember a time, way back in the '70s, when I had an ah-hah moment and it seemed obvious to me that the people around me -- especially my fellow Christians -- had somehow avoided the truth about homosexuality. Out of their in-bred squeamishness and hammered-in desire to look right and be right in the eyes of others, they were failing to see the obvious, the truth that was longingly clear to me . . . because of me. That truth? That God had made us all unique and that for me and many others, that uniqueness meant we were designed, even in His image, to be gay. In other words, if I *feel* this way, I *am* this way and if I *am* this way, I will *be* this way. It was a brief moment of unreal reality. In time, at a time that often seems too late to turn around, the ah-hah turns into oh-no, which can turn into oh-well as we sink into a realization of resignation.

In the simpler '70s -- the tell-it-like-it-is days -- there was little support for that position. Christians, coarsely and clumsily perhaps, were clear on the issue. So was God, through His Word. The evidence was overwhelming and the acceptance of homosexuality was pretty much limited to the non-Christian crowd. Gay and affirming were two words not worthy of a hyphen. As time passed, emboldened ones learned to disguise deep deceits as simple truths.

So let's build a life on feelings. Whoa . . . whoa . . . whoa . . . feelings.

Feelings over truth.

Desires over doctrine.

Collective deceit over self-denial.

Besides, don't you know, don'ts are so depressing. The search is on for birds of a feather, as there's a flock for everything these days.

Years earlier, as a little boy, I took a stroll through a Halloween carnival. I remember a booth where we had to put on blindfolds and reach into buckets and pick up objects and identify them through feeling them. In the environment of the darkening night and the musings of a searching mind, innocent everyday objects became everything from animal guts to eyeballs to elements of torture. That's what they *felt* like. Guesses, right or wrong, were rewarded with candy.

A life built on feelings leads to a slow strangling, trying to swallow intangibles in efforts to convince ourselves that we are on some divine path . . . or, failing that, convince ourselves that there is no divinity. If that be the case, then indeed, why not let feelings rule? We can become rulers over our personally-designed kingdoms, dropping the drawbridge and throwing open the doors to words that match our mind's eye on the things that matter to us . . . and bolting the doors tight to keep out thoughts and ideas -- and truths -- that might hurt . . . our feelings.

I wish it was that innocent: just a little pouting over petty disagreements, rather than people determinedly self-drowning themselves in deep deceit while the keepers of the life-rafts check the equipment and position themselves on the deck to be ready if needed, not aware that misled souls are dropping overboard in silence. Why do we think we need to watch people wear themselves out dashing between the dance partners of the culture and the church until finally we hear some near-death scream of desperation and have to make a decision whether to cut the rope to which they cling or haul them in?

Granted, when I was first struggling with same-sex attraction -- back in the days when such a thing was referred to with slurs and obscene labels -- I never said a word. I dug in and I dug deeper. I soothed my guilt by seeking some kind of justification. I covered shame by projecting purity. I stood on a tightrope doing what was right because I loved God and doing what was wrong because I loved the world too. People pretty much took me at my carefully-crafted word and I moved on, breathing silent sighs of relief, stealthily maneuvering the double life until the inevitable crash and burn. Putting it in relevance to today's society, it now seems like such a tedious spiral, not so much necessary today since we, as Christians, have stood by and watched as pretty much all of the "stigma" of truth has been stripped of any power to persuade people to at least explore the possibility that the path on which they are tiptoeing is not God-ordained.

In the constant celebration of self that inhabits this era of enlightenment, the love of truth has been dismantled by those who have re-labeled it as hate. It's supposed to be that *not* showing love is the clanging of a cymbal, but somehow that has been reversed so that when we look into the eyes of a bewildered and searching man or woman and share the truth, the pro-gay theology bunch -- who have been busy spinning scriptural wishful-thinking -- come pouncing forth, pronouncing disagreement as homophobia and compassion as hate and everyone goes all deaf due to the roar of confusion. It's no wonder -- though the lack of resolve is depressing -- that Christians just look for other problems to solve.

Already we were woefully weak in our efforts to help the uncertain ones who were still trying to find out what the Bible really says and means. The record was dismal even before the pro-gay "theologians" realized they could usurp the position and play with the Word of God just enough to suddenly look like the compassionate ones, curling their pointing fingers to lure the exhausted with promises of finding out finally that they can live as they were intended and shake off all the weight of centuries of Biblical ignorance. It's an empty promise that allows one to live as he wants, restlessly ruling over a kingdom of his own design, sitting on a throne that depends on loyalty and faithfulness to self, always searching for a way to keep himself satisfied as both subject and emperor.

They're not told of the sorrow that eventually unfolds in the life of any Christian who puts anything above God. Yes, we all do it, but in the self-defined kingdom there is no route to repentance. Restoration only comes through the pursuit of pleasure, which, as it turns out, is an endless search to eventual emptiness. Why do we stand helplessly by while the captives we say we want to set free sit nervously around tying greater knots about themselves in a circle of others who nod approval?

I think one of the scariest things about today's pro-gay theology is not that it has all the clarity of a Midwestern corn maze and all the promise of a Mayan temple of sacrifice, but that few people seem to even care. Embracing gay theology for personal relief requires believing Jesus rejected the teachings of His Father. Being as They – Jesus and God -- are One, we might just as well embrace theological schizophrenia. Embracing gay theology requires we believe our personal satisfaction is more valuable than God's truth and that He really said for us to do whatever makes us happy. That should put a new twist on "Love your neighbor as yourself." Embracing gay theology would basically mean that anything Jesus is not quoted as being against, He is for. That would open all kinds of doors, including pedophilia, wife-beating, incest and bestiality. After all, He was silent on those as well, not that every word Jesus ever said was written down. Young Christian men and women are being sucked into the mass of lies like they've tumbled into a pit full of vipers. At the same time, most pastors and church leaders rarely move beyond the promise to pray, sitting back down behind their desks in their offices with their books and bigger issues.

What then should a Christian who struggles with homosexual temptation do?

Open your eyes. -- Examine the scriptures for yourself. Read them in context of the entire expressed Word of God.

Probably more scriptural cherry-picking has taken place regarding homosexuality by both sides than anything else.

Open your mind. -- Pray for wisdom and then read about homosexuality in Leviticus, Romans, 1 Corinthians and 1Timothy. As hard as it is for those who are attracted to and even love someone of the same sex, homosexuality is mentioned only in the context of immoral behavior.

Open your heart. -- God dwells in the hearts of men who give their hearts to Him. He's listening; watching and responding. You think He can't change you if that is the desire of your heart and if you turn your temptation over to Him each time it works to enslave you? Let 1 Corinthians 6:9-11 work in your heart.

Open your door. -- Yes, it's scary to even consider letting people in to know what is troubling you. Find someone you can trust; someone who does not struggle but truly loves both you and the Lord. Pray that God will reveal someone who can walk *with* you and not run *from* you; who can love you and not condemn you; who can forgive you if you fail.

What then should a Christian who does *not* struggle with homosexual temptation do?

Open your eyes. -- We have become so accustomed to diverting our eyes for self-protection that we've not noticed that some of the people who used to walk beside us have been picked off one-by-one. By the time we wake up, they've embraced the empty promises of completeness presented to them as welcome answers to the questions we ignored.

Open your mind. -- I don't mean "have an open mind." I mean learn something. Learn the scriptures. Learn how to apply them accurately. Learn how to support them. Learn how to share them. Learn how to listen to the refutations and reply with the truthful compassion of a Savior who pointed out sin and then helped the sinner stand and walk free.

Open your heart. -- Is your neighbor's son really of no value to you? Is your friend's daughter of no consequence? Is your brother just a passing thought? Should the struggler be a distant memory? Is the sinner for whom repentance is a repeat performance someone we should just brush off? Is the gay man or woman who was once in your circle now to be conveniently redrawn outside the border?

Open your door -- We know the King and we are the kingdom, but we have made it so foreboding that it has become forbidding and those who need it the most are rebuilding it elsewhere, fashioning walls without a true cornerstone. Who can blame Christian men and women, exhausted from the balancing act and the ups-and-downs of the temptations inherent in sexual brokenness for seeking a more welcoming kingdom rather than persistently throwing themselves into our moat? What if we really loved people as much as we say we do? That would be a love that could never be matched by the consumptive love of the other kingdom.

Ears are itching and hearts are twitching. Tears are falling and we're afraid to wipe them away as if the proximity might make us unclean. Soon the crying become the smiling, finally free to be who they were born to be? And we turn away to more fish in the sea.

Pro-gay theology is the myth that keeps on growing, casting a lengthy shadow, yearning to squelch the light of truth.

Move beyond your feelings and share the truth.

CHAPTER 11

OUR INTERIM NAKEDNESS

"Naked I came from my mother's womb, and naked I will depart.
The Lord gave and the Lord has taken away; may the name of the Lord be
praised." -- Job 1:21

My role in the restoration process is to seek it; God's role to give it. My role to accept it; His to affect it. My choice to choose it; His to do it. My role to desire it; His to design it. He imparts unmerited grace; I offer unending praise.

I know that sounds simple, but it can be confusing. Sometimes we put a great deal of effort into self-restoration, as if we can plow through our closets and drawers and then stand in front of a mirror for thirty minutes and apply all the right cover-ups to be convincing. We wink and strike a convincing pose and switch off the flattering light to turn and face . . . realistic life. Other times we turn the restoration over to someone else, an individual who seems to *have* it all together or a group that claims they can *put* it all together for you in 10 not-so-easy-almost-brutal-tough-love steps. Unfortunately, they may judge you more by your practiced poses of self-protection than by your plaintive woes of self-rejection. Depending on how they view you -- from behind masks of rigid self-righteousness or through hearts of tender brokenness -- they do a thumbs-up or thumbs-down, determining whether you are yet broken enough for their repair work to begin. As bad as you know you are, your acceptance of your badness may not look quite good enough for their goodness. Bless you later?

Bless their hearts. It's hard enough for people to deal with their own sins. Do we really have to do the hard work regarding the sins of others? Yes, and with long-suffering to boot. The problem is, most of us are not open about our sinful nature, so when it raises its ugly head, our gracious neighbors find themselves face-to-face with a threatening Cobra and do what comes natural: run for cover.

There's nothing much worse than for those who *really* know you to find out something really bad about you that they really did not know.

What we need is a bit of interim nakedness between the womb and the tomb. Post-discovery transparency is a great thing and certainly helps protect against continued falling, but coming clean beneath the bright lights of exposure can seem a bit late in the relationship-preservation game.

A few years ago ,when I was trying so hard to prove to everyone that I was "all better now," I focused so much energy on looking like things were all right that I had little energy left over to make sure they truly were. That's a surefire plan for relapse. Simply put, if being right for the sake of the ones around us was enough, we would never end up so wrong to begin with. Anyone who has a weakness for an addictive sin has an acquired immunity to those who rightly warn of impending self-destruction. Our yellow-brick road is just a little more yellow and becomes so bright it seems the only path available. Suddenly we're glowing road-kill.

How many times do we as Christians have to say to ourselves and others that God sees all, hears all, knows all before we believe all . . . that? Why do we relegate Him to being a God of retrospection? He has no need of hindsight.

Truth is . . . we're still naked as far as God is concerned. All those earthly shopping binges to wrap ourselves in the latest robes of life -- whether they be righteousness or wretchedness -- are for naught, if we don't come before Him, in a non-literal sense, disrobed. We might fool each other with the latest cover-the-fall fashions, but we'll never fool God.

At some point, most people who struggle with sexual or relational brokenness reach a point where they desperately want to be transformed. Maybe the person they were intended to be has faded so far into the past they don't know even where to start looking. Maybe they have been so derided by people who have long since decided this dog won't hunt when it comes to true change that they have no one to turn to. Maybe they have fooled themselves too many times and spent every penny on tickets on the repentance merry-go-round and they just can't drag themselves into that again without some assurance that the ride might have a different outcome. Maybe, just maybe, they reach a point where it's all "You, God."

Good.

Of course we want things to be right with those we hurt and those we love and those we respect. Of course we want those who turned away to turn back around. Of course we want trust to replace disgust and our present sorrow to be gone tomorrow. Of course we want to count our losses, lick our wounds and come out healed. We want. Remember though, *wanting* is what got us into this mess to begin with, and, if we want restoration, but it does not come because we're expecting it from people who are not ready or able to give it, we can trigger new wants, born of rejection, a sworn enemy of transformation.

Before you start detailing the plans for all that restoration, remember, it's all "You, God." And He's ready, willing and able. Not only that, but God knows what transformation and restoration really look like. If it was up to me, everything I lost because of my years of bowing to sin would come back, just as shiny and new as it was before I tarnished it. As they say, however . . . perhaps "God has a better plan."

My struggle was a lengthy one and I received a lot of advice through the years, some from people who hadn't a clue what I was going through and some from people who had a clue because they'd been through it themselves. One piece of advice they often had in common: "You just need to get your life right with God."

And the smugness in me might roll my eyes and declare that advice to be the epitome of dismissive triteness. When all else fails . . . honey . . . "get right with God."

That's awesome.

Or at least it is if you decide that before all others you're going to get right with the Awesome God who created you . . .

knows you . . . loves you . . . wants you . . . forgives you . . . and will welcome you now and forever if you will only "get right" with Him. What's trite about that?

In the sense of eternity, everything is interim to Him. No matter what you did today, you're still the naked child in your mother's womb and you are already the one who will depart naked. He sees dust-to-dust all at one time, and that's a breadth of knowledge that can certainly see you through the whole journey if you will just . . . "get right with God."

No matter what you fill your life with -- from sin-driven debauchery to servant-driven self-denial -- there will be lonely times and uncertain times and longing times and hurtin' times. We look for places to go and spaces to fill and things to do that will make life more real. For some, life seems just a home-bound journey and for others of us, it works out more like a tumble through a brier-patch. He sees the beginning and the end, the slip, tumble and the struggle to stand.

And He loves you.

That's the truth.

ENCOURAGING WORDS OF TRUTH

CONSIDER HIDING THESE VERSES IN YOUR HEART

For the foolishness of God is wiser than man's wisdom, and the weakness of God is stronger than man's strength.
-- I Corinthians 1:25

"Wait for the Lord. Be strong and let your heart take courage. Yes, wait for the Lord." -- Psalm 27:14

"Come now, let us settle the matter," says the Lord. "Though your sins are like scarlet, they shall be as white as snow; though they are red as crimson, they shall be like wool" -- Isaiah 1:18

The third time He said to him, "Simon son of John, do you love Me?" Peter was hurt because Jesus asked him the third time, "Do you love Me?" He said, "Lord, You know all things; You know that I love you." Jesus said, "Feed My sheep." -- John 21:17

If I speak in the tongues of men or of angels, but do not have love, I am only a resounding gong or a clanging cymbal.
-- I Corinthians 13:1

"If anyone wishes to come after Me, he must deny himself, and take up his cross and follow Me. For whoever wishes to save his life will lose it, but whoever loses his life for My sake and the gospel's will save it. -- Mark 8:34-35

In this you greatly rejoice, though now for a little while you may have had to suffer grief in all kinds of trials. These have come so

that your faith -- of greater worth than gold, which perishes even though refined by fire -- may be proved genuine and may result in praise, glory and honor when Jesus Christ is revealed.
-- I Peter 1: 6-7

"Ask and it will be given to you; seek and you will find; knock and the door will be opened to you. For everyone who asks receives; he who seeks finds; and to him who knocks, the door will be opened." -- Matthew 7: 7-8

Then He called the crowd to Him along with His disciples and said: "Whoever wants to be My disciple must deny themselves and take up their cross and follow Me." -- Mark 8:34

"Come to Me, all you who are weary and burdened, and I will give you rest." -- Matthew 11:28

Finally, brothers and sisters, whatever is true, whatever is noble, whatever is right, whatever is pure, whatever is lovely, whatever is admirable -- if anything is excellent or praiseworthy -- think about such things. -- Philippians 4:8

Jesus replied: "'Love the Lord your God with all your heart and with all your soul and with all your mind.' This is the first and greatest commandment. And the second is like it: 'Love your neighbor as yourself.' All the Law and the Prophets hang on these two commandments." -- Matthew 22:36-40

Speak and act as those who are going to be judged by the law that gives freedom, because judgment without mercy will be shown to anyone who has not been merciful. Mercy triumphs over judgment! -- James 2:12

"And such were some of you. But you were washed, but you were sanctified, but you were justified in the name of the Lord Jesus and by the Spirit of our God." – I Corinthians 6:11

For the time will come when people will not put up with sound doctrine. Instead, to suit their own desires, they will gather around them a great number of teachers to say what their itching ears want to hear. They will turn their ears away from the truth and turn aside to myths. -- I Timothy 4:3-4

"Naked I came from my mother's womb, and naked I will depart. The Lord gave and the Lord has taken away; may the name of the Lord be praised." -- Job 1:21

HOPE

CHAPTER 12

ALL THE LIVELONG DAY

On darker nights and somber days when I wander on my own
I think through things that bother me as if the answer's known
Somewhere deep inside myself where broken memories lie
And I believe once more that I'll be fine if *I* give it one more try.

It's when I step outside myself that I begin to see,
Because in love the Lord Himself begins to show to me
The lies, the tricks, the subtleties to which I tend to cling,
The choruses of celebrating self that culture says to sing.

A song composed of justifying what we want or do
Of self-indulgence, satisfying what seems right to you
Instead of truly living out a life that God Himself designed
Culture's song says freedom comes from leaving Him behind.

Alone I peer down deep inside for answers not found there
Despite advice to search my soul from those who feign to care.
The truth is, only Christ can tell me what I need to know,
For He alone can fully see what lies within my soul.

When I was building a life around secret sexual
satisfaction, I did not have the luxury of thinking it was okay. As a
Christian, I knew it wasn't, and I almost envied people who were
sure it was, at least for them, because I pictured them as blissfully
going along in ignorance, free from the guilt and shame I brought
upon myself. I was unable to sanction my actions with self-
deserving platitudes, such as "God made me this way." I had to

63

settle for plain old deceit in the effort to get away with a life of self-indulgence. Brick by brick, I built a wall over which I would only occasionally -- with increasing infrequency -- peer above to see the truth beyond. The wall got longer and longer to where there seemed no way around it, taller and taller to a height beyond climbing and I hunkered down behind it. This was to be me. I would find some way to survive in a repetitive cycle of refusing God and refusing self . . . but mostly refusing reality. In truth, it *wasn't* me because it required me to not be His. And I already was. His, that is.

Bricks held together with flawed and flimsy mortar have a tendency to tumble under the weight of truth. The wreckage almost destroyed me and when He rescued me from the dust and debris, most of the ones I had walled out had fled the tragic scene. Even repentance is not insurance against consequence. I was back into the light, but the view was drastically different. We can even find ourselves longing for the comfort of the self-satisfaction we once saw as freedom.

It's not.

Anything built on secrecy and deception is . . . a wall. And if we are the builders, we're on the wrong side of that wall.

I woke up one morning with the lyrics to *I've Been Working on the Railroad* rolling around in my head. It made no sense at the moment, but I did. I know . . . Texans took the tune and used it for *The Eyes of Texas Are upon You*, and I know a lot of people down there, but . . . it was the railroad song that invaded my sleep and left me wondering why I woke up to, not, for instance, *Amazing Grace*, but "strumming on the old banjo." I kept repeating the line "All the livelong day." We don't much say "livelong" any more, unless perhaps you're a trekkie, and then it's two words: "Live long . . . and prosper." Different meaning altogether.

Sometimes I think the journey through sexual brokenness is much like working on the railroad, laying down tracks along the open landscape that will soon be burdened with massive freight that can only go where the tracks lead. It becomes then, not an adventure, not a discovery, but a fixed trip to the designated end of the line where the cars are emptied, filled again, and sent traveling back down the same old track. Nothing changes on the track, unless by some ill-fated fortune a misplaced bit of debris derails the train or, worse, another freight-hauler appears on the same track and your fixed journeys collide into chaos.

Sexual brokenness is just a same-old-same-old search for something that is not there because it lies outside the reach of the track on which the broken travel. Only when you jump the track does your view change enough to realize that a better land lies away from the back-and-forth-and-once-again track on which you cross almost unnoticed, other than an occasional warning of the whistle hauntingly drifting away from the tracks into the lonely night. Even the whistle sounds the same every time it sounds.

Sometimes someone hears it. God *always* does.

Christians who struggle with sexuality should have the same desire to be what God wants them to be as Christians who do not struggle. After all, though sexuality seems exclusively scary, every Christian struggles with something that threatens to separate him from Him. We should not go around patting ourselves on the back, proclaiming victory over something the other guy struggles with. That's just so . . . un-Christian, you know?

I remember when I was in college and in the Lambda Chi fraternity. I would see frat brothers downing drinks almost like it was a competition to see who would first kiss the carpet. I never drank. Not once.

I have seen people whose lives have disintegrated into gasping for air with a cigarette in hand. I never smoked. Not once.

I have seen the pictures of meth addicts, their future as shriveled as their faces. I never experimented with drugs. Never had to decide whether or not to inhale. Not once.

I never wanted to drink . . . to smoke . . . to shoot up or light up or snort down. Not once. Ahhh . . . what victory. Over something by which I was never tempted. Where is my well-deserved pat on the back? I don't think so. What arrogance to point a finger and shake my head at those who tripped upon curiosity and found themselves drowning in addictive temptation.

I am inclined to think that we have trapped ourselves on a one-way track because we have tied ourselves to the idea of "choice." He made a choice. She chose to be a lesbian. He chose to build a life of pornographic fantasy. He focused in on adultery and pursued it. When we proclaim the sexually-broken as just another victim of a choice, we elevate the alternative -- homosexuality, pornography, adultery -- to just another alternative some humans prefer. That may work for regular old humans, but it won't work when we are talking about Christians. It's a smokescreen that envelops all in a gray shade and mere shadow of freedom, a battle between the "I can't help myself," and the "You darn sure can." The battle between "I" and "you."

Both are off the hook. One gives in. The other moves on. All sigh.

We really have only once *choice* if we are to survive this world and stay on track to the next one, eternity with Christ, who has heard our whistle and is waving His welcome . . . home. The choice is to follow God's will and not our own. And to know the Father's will, all we need do is know His Word and follow it. All the livelong day.

Christ does not give up on us. He does not abandon us. He can't, because He said He would not. People do both, and most will, if you are not going their way, whether it be on a path of self-indulgence or sanctification. People may choose to turn toward you or away from you based on what you do and what they think. I'm not judging, just pointing out another reason why we have to realize it is in Christ alone we cross the land. If you are depending on anyone or anything else right now, well then you just haven't unfolded enough of the map yet. A few more detours and you'll see.

Have you been on this train long enough yet? If so, while it's just an old railroad song, pay attention to this line: "Can't you hear the Captain calling?"

All the livelong day.

CHAPTER 13

A THOUSAND SLEEPLESS NIGHTS

Are you sleeping, are you sleeping?
Brother John, Brother John?
Morning bells are ringing, morning bells are ringing
Ding ding dong, ding ding dong.

"I have no peace, no quietness; I have no rest, but only turmoil."
-- Job 3:21

I love the promise of peace in each new day, but I will not forget the dark of the sleepless nights of sorting through a sin-dominated past seeking the softness of a forgiving dawn, which came only through the freedom of finding grace, the source of hope.

The dark nights would end with tints of orange and red and brightening gray as through the bedside window I would see the sun struggling to find its shape along the horizon, eventually freeing itself from the trap of trees, giving them color and sliding, round and victoriously glowing, into an ever-bluer sky . . . as I awoke. Or did I? Awake . . . or just get up?

It was time to free myself from the traps that entangled my mind throughout the night, and myself seek shape, trying to move beyond my own horizon and out into the sky, less-anchored by the weight of endless thoughts which overwhelm the night. A little distraction, please? A shower, some TV, a bowl of soggy sameness, the gathering of the things which make the day seem right, an exit to the car with a nod to the now-dominating sun.

Day. Awake. Up. On. For hours now, I will accumulate thoughts and interactions, welcome distractions, and line up the dos of this and that and mark them down as dones . . . and then the sun will also be done . . . and the day will fade into another sleepless night. Perhaps if I counted them instead of sheep? 990 . . . 991 . . . 992 . . . 993 . . . 994 . . . 995 . . . 996 . . . 997 . . . 998 . . . 999.

Not all in a row of course and not all for the same reasons, but all there: a thousand sleepless nights, some spent driving around, some watching a steady declining-in-value spiraling of television, others puffing up and pounding down pillows in periods of pondering or lying still in the silence of lamenting, turned toward a window beyond which nothing moves, reinforcing the hopelessness of going nowhere.

G'morning.

Maybe it was not, or is not, that way for you in your battle with sexual sin. But, I remember it that way. A series of sleepless nights would lead to a sleep-filled night not sent by peace, but evidence of exhaustion. On and on. Searching for something and yet expending all the energy it would have taken to claim it if found. Hanging in there by day, giving in by night to the mix of memories and bad moments and excuses and cover-ups and denials and desires and loneliness and regrets tied together to the oh . . . the awful unfairness of it all?

Woe is me. Mercy . . . what light through yonder window breaks?

God called the light "day," and the darkness he called "night." And there was evening, and there was morning -- the first day. -- Genesis 1:5

And there it happened. The first separation, this of day and night, more evidence of a Creator who could make all out of nothing. The first day . . . and before all sleepless nights.

Separation is not an altogether pleasant word. It speaks of distance. Of walls. Of isolation. Of taking away. Of . . . sleeplessness in sorrow or suspense on the sad side of a bridgeless gap.

We are not hesitant to remind each other that sin separates. Before, during or after, we, at some point, pull the string that closes the veil between us and God, as if He, who deftly divided dark from light cannot see through to me and you. We're hiding from the ever-present.

We're the ones who welcome the descending of the curtain.

But your iniquities have separated you from your God; your sins have hidden His face from you, so that He will not hear. -- Isaiah 59:2

Truth is, this separation from God because of our sexual sin has severe consequences in our attempts to stumble through the life we really want. It's out there . . . but we are somewhere "in here," separated, in so many, many ways. To name just a few:

1. From God -- This is the big one because we know He's always there; He never forsakes; He knows all; sees all; never leaves or fails to love. But . . . we fail to call on Him and descend instead into sighs of separation.

2. From self -- How many times did it almost seem like I was standing by the side of the road watching my own descent into darkness, removed from it but wrapped in it? I would pursue and run, fight and surrender, all at the same time. Satisfy myself and point an incriminating finger simultaneously. Sinner.

3. From others -- It's not true that what you don't know won't hurt you. In fact, the opposite is often true. In our efforts to protect ourselves from others while we dress the welts of our sin, we lessen what brought us together and reinforce what keeps us apart. Guarded and secretive, we have to either create something unreal to fill in the gaps, or we have to distance ourselves from those who we believe might reject us if they really knew us. There's a flip side truth to all of this. Some do, and that's a very painful separation.

4. From reality -- The only way you can justify doing something that your heart and soul and God-sent wisdom tells you is wrong, is to create an alternate reality in which you cling to the hope of survival. It's me-based. "This is right for *me*." "This is how God made *me*." "I can't help it; this is *me*." "You don't really care about *me*."

5. From truth -- That's what the devil did with Eve when he said "Surely God didn't mean . . . " And, surely God did. That's what the sexually-broken do when they say "Surely the Bible doesn't really mean . . . " But it does. So, the choice is to accept truth or embrace lies. One seems easier and binds you day and night forever. The other frees you.

6. From healing pain -- This one is confusing because the more we do to protect ourselves from pain, the greater it eventually hurts. Perhaps this one is actually separation-saturation. We seek the self-medication of sexual sin and then, when done, we feel the pain of self-betrayal, which is much more painful than self-denial would ever have been.

7. From hope -- Nothing is as defeating as giving in to sin. This war seems made of endless battles. Most men and women enveloped in the surge of sexual sin see no reinforcements left or right and surrender one by one their weapons in a sense of hopelessness. They cannot do it on their own, but choose to out of fear of being all alone in revelation.

8. From love -- I know there were times when some who wanted to love me could not figure out how because I was not always the me they thought they knew and loved. Fences of protection I would build around me worked like filters. Two-way filters. Gongs resounding from both directions.

9. From mercy -- Mercy comes in response to an honest plea, a surrender. When we cling to our sin, battle-worn and weary, saving what energy we have to assure we do not lose that sin we so align with, we are not seen as surrendering or pleading, we're seen as determinedly self-destructive, which may not be true at all, as we are more likely bound-addictive. Still, mercy hesitates.

10. From forgiveness -- True forgiveness seems so demanding to the sexually-broken, as the right response is to clean up your act. Life is more bearable with a chip on your shoulder which makes it easier to spread the blame a bit. "I am so . . . *judged.*" God forgives. That's it. And yes, accepting forgiveness does produce within us the desire for confession and repentance . . . but that's what we want. It's not demanding; it's freeing.

And so it goes. Sin separates, from God, from self, from others, reality and truth, from healing pain and hope, from love and mercy . . . and forgiveness. And then from peace and wholeness, the great desire of the broken.

Interestingly, for those who think that sexual sin elevates us to some higher level of separation, it does not. It's sin. Every head on every pillow is in danger of the parade of sleepless nights from separation, for "all have sinned." The Bible tells us so.

The big question is, if you are separated, what should you do? *Jump.* Just like you would if you were standing on one side of a river a thousand miles long and twenty feet wide and there was no way to cross unless you jumped in first and began to swim, one stroke at a time.

1. Approach God in prayer. He answers.

2. Confront yourself. You will survive.

3. Be honest with others. Those who know of love . . . will love you. Those who don't are sinning by not and the separation may not be your fault after all.

4. Accept reality. It's really not about you. It's all about Him.

5. Embrace the truth. God's Word is for your good, not for your defeat.

6. Acknowledge the pain. God's mercy is never-ending. You've been hurt; you have hurt others. God is not unfamiliar with the pain of His people and He can heal your wounds if you will surrender them.

7. Have hope. Hope is not a tangible thing, but it is a powerful presence. And, if your hope is in the Lord, it is a permanent one. Quit giving it up or losing it.

8. Share love. Take it from others; give it to others. Don't reject the love of others because it's so hard to love yourself. Let love lead the way.

9. Cry out for mercy . . . and mean it. Yes, it is a natural response when we have flung ourselves into the pits of mud to cry out for a strong hand. True surrender is a shunning of the mud in response to a shower of redemption.

10. Forgive. Yourself. And forgive those who do not forgive you. And ask again for forgiveness.

God is a hands-on healer. When we separate ourselves from Him and from the ones He might use in our lives, we allow our sin to be the determiner of our lives.

Wake up. A thousand sleepless nights are enough.

CHAPTER 14

BUILDING BRIDGES ON A LONELY TRAIL

"It is finished."

Can there be more satisfying words? Said in quiet resolve as a father steps back from a swing set in the yard, an artist scoots back from a painting, a writer pushes away from a keyboard, a seamstress sews the final seam, a final test is taken, or a silent prayer is lifted. When we sense completion, we spread our arms like a blessing, then rest our hands on our hips to take the moment in before life moves on.

Life moves on? I thought we were finished.

I thought about these things as I chopped and sawed my way through thick brush and dead trees, spiders scattering and unseen creatures of the woods keeping their distance in the shadows of the thick trees around me. My arms were scratched, my clothes drenched in sweat, my back itching from mosquito bites, my mind tired of the question: "why am I doing this?"

I had started this trail through the woods more than 10 years ago. I renewed my commitment about five years ago. This trail had always had a beginning, a couple of twists and turns and an abrupt ending at a small creek, beyond which the daunting cluttered undergrowth grew stronger and thicker year after year.

And then I finally crossed the creek. With better tools and a clearer mind, I hacked and sawed and pulled and raked and the crackling of old dead branches piled on top of each other from the tossing of storms and the passing of years eventually gave way to a soft padding beneath my feet, rich dirt and decaying leaves. A little sun sifting through the trees lighted the path and highlighted the green around me.

My path twisted around the more formidable trees and found its way . . . back to the creek at a wider spot, a path of water trickling slowly down the middle of the muddy banks pocked with deer tracks and home to turtles. Now, with just a couple of bridges, the trail will be done.

Empty.

Out of sight.

Invisible to almost everyone.

But done.

I know for sure that I did not know where my trail in life would lead two years ago when I left my job at AT&T, retreated back into the darkness of shame, emerged into the light of transparency, began writing this blog, wrote a book and trusted God to somehow do what I had never trusted him to do before. Build the bridge. Get me to the end of this trail.

In my life, like in the woods, I had long had a trail and had worn it deep from pacing back and forth upon it, committing and retreating. The beginning of the trail was as familiar as the back of my hand. The point at which I would always stop was worn deep from my screeching halts at the banks of the creek -- not a mighty river -- but just a stream that turned me back to try again another day. I think I always thought that as long as I could keep the creek in sight, I would someday have the resolve to cross it. I could see the other side, but it seemed a jump too far. It was too thick. I needed tools. I needed help. I needed a bridge.

I spent a lot of time trying to think of who might help me build that bridge and I got angry, longing for volunteers, but I also got honest and realized I'd worn that pool of people thin. Too many times I had trekked to the creek and turned back, and the hope of the trail's completion had faded for them. I thought also that there were some who should just be obligated to help: ministers and family members, sons and daughters not allowed to just give up . . . but I realized they had come to a conclusion, with reason, that *I* had given up, so why not they? And I got angry at myself because I had no list to work through; the names were all scratched off. Of course, my wife's name was still there . . . but I wanted to clear this trail and build this bridge and then walk it with her . . . not ask her to bear the machete, which she was always ready to do.

Since I didn't know, really, what to expect out of those years, I was a bit surprised to feel I had not met my expectations. Like the trail in the woods, the one in life takes constant maintenance, a clearing of the weeds and a chopping back of the vines which like to slyly creep in from the sides. And, like the trail in the woods, it is not widely traveled by companions of the past. I thought some who had seen it lay unfinished might have come back to see the progress and walk the path to see its end. It's a peaceful trail, but a bit more quiet than I might have presumed it would be.

Some Christians will see some day that their stone-throwing has driven countless souls back from the creek side. Other Christians will have much to answer for when their eyes are someday opened and they realize that their pride at not throwing stones was only a partial following of Jesus. Jesus was willing to stretch a hand out to the one who would have been stoned to help her stand again, take her out of the dust, look her in the eyes, offer forgiveness and hope.

I think those of us who strive to overcome sexual brokenness have to realize at some point that not every bridge we build replaces ones we burned.

The question, then, is what to do with loneliness so it becomes not a trigger for sexual backtracking, but a beckoning to spiritual backpacking.

When I forget who said He will never leave me, I dwell on those who said they would and did. When I wonder where everyone else is, I forget that He is with me always. When I get lonely, I forget I am never only.

Be thankful if you have someone to walk with. But . . . nice as it is to know, you and I both know that even with a co-walker, we are no match for the darkest part of the path.

Not you. Not me. Only He. He who gives us strength. He who takes away fear.

Be strong and courageous. Do not be afraid or terrified because of them, for the Lord your God goes with you; He will never leave you nor forsake you. -- Deuteronomy 31:6

The trail looks a lot better now, doesn't it?

For I am convinced that neither death nor life, neither angels nor demons, neither the present nor the future, nor any powers, neither height nor depth, nor anything else in all creation, will be able to separate us from the love of God that is in Christ Jesus our Lord. -- Romans 8:38-40

Nor anything else in all creation? Not judgmental words? Not harsh rejections? Not bewilderment? Not shame? Not guilt? Not misunderstandings? Not temptations? Not failings? Not loneliness?

If you are out there wandering along on an all-too-familiar path, wishing you could jump the creek or cut a new route that did not circle back to no-where, or your mind tires of the question: "Why am I doing this?," remember that God's Word is infallible and His grace is beyond exhausting. If you're walking alone, it's because you are denying His presence.

I don't like being lonely. In my own estimation of restoration, everyone would be back by now and we'd be having picnics by the side of the creek, while the grandchildren scurried up and down the trail discovering all of creation.

In trust, though, I can keep walking this trail for what it is. It has a beginning; it has an end. And there are bridges now.

CHAPTER 15

BY WHAT ARE YOU SURROUNDED?

I tire at times of wondering what is happening to me
Who I was and who am I and who I'm meant to be.
Like going in and out a door with choices in between
Choices close and clear now, but for so long so unseen.

I was here and I was there but I was never anywhere,
Surrounded by a self that I could never dare to share.
wondering turns to wandering; we're not where we want to be,
Self-surrounded, not surrendered, and unable to be free.

Looking out, we reach for those who claim to want us free
But box us in and see us as they think we'll always be.
Look up, the God of Wonders, makes our wondering cease
The only God of love and grace; He gives the wanderer peace.

How can you be lost and alone and yet surrounded by a smothering presence?

How can you be so in need of insight from others and yet drowning in it at the same time?

How can you stay perched upon a fine line between hope and hopelessness so long your body aches, your soul cries out and your voice comes back like a whiplash against your mind?

How can you find yourself in this place where up and down and back and forth merge into a motionless state where at one moment a gentle nudge could send you sailing or a tiny word could send you flailing?

How?

By finding yourself, through no choice of your own, in the confusing and confounding cocoon where Christians who struggle with gripping sexual issues curl up and mentally confine themselves, fighting too much on their own a temptation with tentacles that wind around and in, like some alien invader who lets you seem okay outside but claims the inner territory set aside for the soul . . . and wages a battle for control. Unfortunately, many Christians who might be equipped to help you are so entranced by what seems like a hideous hitchhiking alien that they don't see the heart of the host.

Just try revealing yourself to someone who is not equipped to handle the news. Or, worse yet, take some unfortunate step or stumble, succumbing to sexual temptation. "You're surrounded." It gets very hard sometimes to tell the difference between the well-meaning and the mean. The loving and the leaving. The help and the hate.

'Tis a dilemma. Despite all the hard work of numerous para-church organizations and the eye-opening crusades of culture, most churches and many Christians still border on clueless. Finding out that a "brother" or "sister" struggles with homosexuality or, even worse, has been in a homosexual lifestyle and wants out, is as likely to bring a "Get thee behind me, Satan," as an offer to stand beside you.

My harshness is not based strictly on personal experience, but even more so on the recounting of others who have felt their inner pain expounded upon by those they turned to for answers. in the absence of answers, fingers point. Prayers are said, yes, but followed up quickly by checklists to see if they've been answered promptly. Admitting to sexual sin is like volunteering for a Christian-brother probation list. Rather than "They'll know we are Christians by our love," it becomes "We'll know you're a Christian by your change." And, if the change is not clear in their eyes, you can swiftly move into a new category: condemned.

Can. I did not say, *will*. In fact, I have discovered, perhaps through the longevity of my own struggle, that there are many Christians who do not struggle with sexuality, but see sexual sin as sin, something with which they themselves admit familiarity. Familiarity with and recognition of their own sins led them to realize it is God that heals, not angry church leaders or hurt members who are more inclined to ponder the momentary impact on them of your sin than the death it is dealing you day-to-day. The response I hear from more and more Christians regarding reaching out to the sexually-broken is "this is needed."

But . . . what about when people demean you or doubt you?

If you are truly seeking repentance, not playing on the edges, but striding straight into the middle of the battlefield, arming yourself as best you know how, honest before God . . . then dismiss their demeaning and their doubt. You'll have enough of your own without laying awake at night and dwelling on theirs. Sometimes we need a little separation from the self-righteous in order to get a glimpse of the reality of righteousness.

But . . . what about when people accuse you falsely and label you unjustly?

I'm not going to say "blessed are you when . . . " because obviously they're labeling you out of what they know and believe about you because of what they may have seen or heard from you yourself or from others who are inclined to spread the news of your sinful state, whether it be past or present. False accusations usually come from fear, ignorance or susceptibility to the devil's schemes. He would like nothing more than for you to spend your time and energy battling others rather than battling him and the temptations he will pile up before you during the distraction of defending yourself from the ones who point. Again . . . . sometimes we have to move away from people to find God outside their shadow.

Teach me your way, Lord; lead me in a straight path because of my oppressors. Do not turn me over to the desire of my foes, for false witnesses rise up against me, spouting malicious accusations.
-- Psalm 27:11-12

Let the Lord lead.

But . . . what about those people who think you cannot change?

Pray that *they* do, and that they discover the depth of God's grace and do more than pay lip-service to His unlimited power. The truth is, many of these people believe in change for almost everything else, but impose their own doubts on God when it comes to sexual brokenness. It goes on the "yeah, but not this, list," as though God has asked them for advice on how He should wield His mighty pen of restoration as he draws the course upon which we tread. I myself have been guilty of looking at those who label me beyond repair and saying to myself: "They'll never change." God forgive our opposing declarations of dismissal.

And that is what some of you were. But you were washed, you were sanctified, you were justified in the name of the Lord Jesus Christ and by the Spirit of our God. -- 1 Corinthians 6:11

"Were" equals change.

But . . . what should I tell someone if I fall? Won't they just say "I told you so?"

So.

Satan would much rather you focus on what they are saying so you won't see what God is doing. Through our trials and temptations, even when we stumble and fall, we learn about His grace, His provision, our salvation, the patience of our Lord, and the strong hand that reaches out. Yes, "I told you so," is painful. For every stumbling sinner, there are a multitude of prophets. Again, if you are truly repentant and you are truly praying, focus not on the "I told you so's" of men, but on the "I will's" of God.

I lift up my eyes to the mountains -- where does my help come from? My help comes from the Lord, the Maker of heaven and earth. He will not let your foot slip -- He who watches over you will not slumber; -- Psalm 121:1-3

Our help comes from the Lord.

But . . . I feel like I'm always starting over.

This is not a race. We don't spring from the blocks at the start of a pistol and try to beat everyone to redemption. We walk with the Lord, and pray for Him to set the pace and stay beside us all the way. He doesn't rush to the finish line and say, "Oh well."

79

He takes each step with us until we get there and then He says "Well done." We don't start at the same place, run the same course, mark the same time, but we have the same Savior walking beside us as those who seek repentance for sins far removed from sexuality. Their path is different and perhaps just as hard, but the finish line is for all. Don't turn your back on the finish line and turn around and start over. Go on. Every time you get back up, the finish line is little bit closer if you keep heading in the same direction.

Some have . . . given up and given in. Others *think* they have, but will find out later that their love of the Lord calls them back out of falseness and out on the course to complete the next lap. The only giving up and giving in we need to do is to give up ourselves and give in to God. What an awesome God who does not scratch us from the team, who looks beyond our inadequacy to see, Who helps us up and on, seeking the good soil for our impoverished roots.

But the seed on good soil stands for those with a noble and good heart, who hear the word, retain it, and by persevering produce a crop.
-- Luke 8:15

Perseverance produces.

To whom are you listening? By what are you surrounded? Sometimes we listen too much. Sometimes we enlist soldiers from among the armor-less. As a struggler, it is very important that we ourselves know the Word of God so we can know to whom we should listen. When you hear people -- well-meaning or not -- proclaiming a way that is not the Lord's, then you are in serious danger of being cast into some very bad soil. The very ones who plant you there will be the ones who later lament your lack of fruit and get anxious to yield the pruning shears.

Sometimes perseverance comes through clearing. Clearing out the clinging vines that choke the progress of growth that everyone -- including you -- wants to chart.

Bear fruit. That first grape is the sign of an orchard on the horizon.

CHAPTER 16

SO WHERE DO WE GO FROM HERE?

We once had guarded secrets we determined not to tell.
Words, thoughts and deeds we would share in desperate prayer.
The secrets slept and crept beneath the rocks on which we fell,
But once emerged, revealed, those secrets suddenly weren't there.

But what's beyond healed secrets if the truth is not accepted?
If haunts of past decisions wrap the future like a wall?
If cries for forgiveness and hopes for renewal are openly rejected?
If restoration's trapped beneath those rocks and mercy flees the
call?

Can we not see each other as God sees you and me
And drop the stones and lift instead His mercy and His grace?
Can we not lay aside our hurt, our memories, our pride
So truth and love can sweep away the walls that still divide?

My faith in Christ tells me someway, somehow, someday we can,
That redemption's strength can free us all to open ears and eyes
So when I see the arms still folded, the judging glare of man
I choose God's grace, the gift of love, from He who heard my cries.

The words "So where do we go from here?" can make the
memories flow, flooding me with the undeniable reality of some
really bad answers to that question, sometimes in part because
there really was not, at the time, much consideration for the "we"
part of it. It was too often more of an "I" question, refusing to

realize that there are very few places we go without dragging others along with us like resistant back-seat children rolling their eyes and protesting as we pull into yet another roadside attraction on a less-than-rollicking ride down some never-ending highway.

I do remember that my Dad, when I was a little boy, was as interested as I was in the roadside tin-roofed run-down buildings that boasted of the world's largest snake or a two-headed alligator or an albino something-or-another. Those were good stops. The frequent stops at places like Dusty's Drinking Hole, kids left sitting in a dusty parking lot in a sticky-seated car, were not so good. We always knew that "where do we go from here?" would include a stop for beer.

No one travels alone, regardless of intent. Those of us who have, for one reason or another, struggled with one of the many forms of sexual brokenness, may have made many attempts to internalize it, but it splashes like careless bleach on those around us, taking a little color here and there from their lives and leaving a mark of our presence. Addictions are not targeted solely at the one decaying in the center; they reach out to stain the ones who care . . . and sometimes slowly decide not . . . to care.

One spring day when I was in junior high, I came home from school to find my mother standing in the living room of our little duplex. My stepfather had found us after a lengthy absence and had come by to bust up all the furniture and pull down the drapes, leaving our shattering exposed. "Where do we go from here?"

I remember when a best-friend friendship, which had evolved into something it never should have, imploded as we discovered we were making different choices . . . each of which would lead to struggles within, but would separate us permanently. A friendship became instead a wall. "Where do we go from here?"

I remember sitting in our living room surrounded by my children confronting me with more evidence of my corrupted double-life of surrender to temptation, eyes pleading for explanation, filling with condemnation, growing colder and more distant with each moment. Eventually, when all the truth had been spread out like layers of dirt burying me to near suffocation, I could only wonder . . . "Where do we go from here?"

I remember sitting in a cold, bare room at the county jail, keeping the distance between my shame and the shame of those surrounding me, thinking of all the loss to come and asking . . . "Where do we go from here?"

And perhaps the most searing memory of all comes not from a truth, but from a lie so sinister and evil that it set the moments of life's goodness to falling like dominoes until finally at the end of the train of falling there is only silence and separation, lives twisted by twisted lies. Desperate attempts at digging truth from beneath the debris of lies seemed hopeless enough, but the thimble threads of the lie became like reinforced steel in the hands of the bitter who should know better. The deep hurt and trust my children bore at this point was, I believe, encouraged and reinforced by overblown, meddling "told-you-sos" carelessly crafting their chaotic intrusion "out of love." Leaders blinded by their own misguided brilliance and over-stated purity of perspective, led us finally to that familiar question . . . "Where do we go from here?"

It seemed like in most cases, the unspoken word has always been "further down." Some travelers are headed for Pike's Peak. I seemed intent on making my way to the bottom of Devil's Den, descending with a blindfold on. Who needs a guide when it's all just one direction?

But it's not. There is never just one direction, and there is always a guide. The hope lies in the question . . . "Where do WE go from here?"

When we begin a journey in search of freedom and change, we have expectations. Some are quickly realized; others, perhaps a bit unrealistic, take longer. Over-riding all is ever-strengthening hope -- once hidden in darkness and stunted by the separation sin presents -- that now grows and turns this traveler out of the cavern to see the peak on the horizon.

I sought most of all to confront this struggle, to drag it out into the open, into the light, deprive it of the nourishment of deception, divide it by sharing it, conquer it by dividing it, submit it to the truth of trust and obey . . . rather than submitting myself to distrust and decay. Confront I did. Conquer completely? Of that, I can not boast; the mind is ever in need of further discipline.

But . . . I trust. And, a temptation becomes . . . a temptation . . . and not a taskmaster.

As for the unrealistic?

I'll be honest. When my job as Oklahoma chief of staff at AT&T ended, I did not know where I was going. Having always worked somewhere from about the age of 12, I knew I would work somewhere, probably until I'm 112. It didn't happen as I would have expected "Where do we go from here?" became just "here." Home. So . . . I trust.

I thought I would soon be able to share in joy about the restoration of my family, that I would say that I had been able to see my grandchildren, would have been forgiven and given the opportunity to replace the thick walls of deception with thin panes of transparency. Nope. Not yet. "Where do we go from here?" is still unclear. My daughter Lauren backpacked through Asia, perhaps wondering the same thing: "Where do we go from here?," writing of her own journey. Zachary continues to raise his family, the children growing up and growing strong, out of sight. Donovan fought for freedom as an Army Ranger and now protects his city as a police officer as his family also grows. Patrick, also a police officer, protects others and his children. Russell studies and writes and continues on his own quest to know not just where we go now but the truth of where we came from. God sees all . . . and I trust.

I anticipated restored relationships with the churches which disciplined me and removed me from fellowship, and that the leadership there would re-visit my life and allow me the opportunity to seek reconciliation. Nope. "Where do we go from here?" is clearly still not there. Their silence speaks of the emptiness in their own hearts.

So . . . in the face of all these uncompleted expectations, why is there so much hope?

Because, the word in the question is *"We."* It is not *"I."* As individuals, we often think we know where God will go with us when we take His hand. We declare our trust, our yieldedness, but our shortsightedness guides our expectations and we forget that the Timeless One has those plans He told us about, and, if we walk with Him, that's where He intends to go: back to the plans He has for us.

"For I know the plans I have for you," declares the Lord, "plans to prosper you and not to harm you, plans to give you hope and a future."
-- Jeremiah 29:11

Can there be a more comforting verse for the struggler and the stumbler? Can there be a better promise for the broken?

God doesn't wonder or question or ponder or weigh. He "knows." All.

God doesn't conjure, or consider, or react, or re-think. He has "plans." In place.

God doesn't quick-fix or pull out a one-fits-all remedy. He has plans for "you." You alone.

And, while we sit in dismay, picking scabs of carnage off our scraped knees and counting our losses, God says this tailored-made-for-me plan is . . . to "prosper" me.

And while we know we are reviled by some and the subject of others' tortured thoughts and, as in my case, turned over for the destruction of the flesh . . . God, who loves me and knows me and has . . . plans . . . for me says those plans will not harm me.

He says those plans will give me . . . hope.

Best of all, for the person in the spin-cycle of "Where will we go from here?" he has an answer. His plans give us a "future."

That's what I want. Heaven knows . . . and pretty much everyone else in the world it seems . . . I have a past. I want a future.

Yes . . . I still have expectations, but they are based on hope and prayer now, not a mind-numbing struggle to put it all back together, to bring everyone home, to see the lie surrendered on the altar of truth. My expectations are built on God-sustained hope, not self-draining struggle. My expectations are wrapped in the trust that God's Word is true and unbending: "I have plans for *you*." Knowing that, God, You can have my expectations . . . and where they don't fit Your plans, discard them and replace them with Your perfect ones.

If God has plans, He also has surprises, for our minds cannot conceive the good He has in store for us . . . if we trust. And obey.

Amazing words from God bear repeating: "I have plans for you."

For you too. I picture a cavernous room that stretches throughout eternity and a little nook that has a perfectly-preserved scroll on which His plans for you are down in great detail. Not discarded. Not given-up-on. Not removed. Not dusty, as He looks at them daily. Just ready.

Not on the plan at the moment? Stooped beneath the weight of unrealized expectations? A bit tattered from the target practice of the one-eyed ones who wink with the plank-filled eye and take aim with the other? God knows.

So . . . .where will you go from here?

CHAPTER 17

SHOULD WE REALLY BURN THE BRIDGES?

I woke up this morning and I was still here.
Unwanted thoughts banished were once again near.
I can leave them with yesterday and travel only so far,
And when I wake up, once again, here they are.

These sturdy old bridges that connect to our past,
Composed of old memories determined to last,
Have an entrance in twilight, and an exit in dawn.
But across these old bridges we learn to move on.

As we move, we look back and the road starts to fade,
But the bridges of decisions once carelessly made,
Stand strong, a reminder of where we have been,
And where we want never to travel again.

Though some we love stand on the bridge's far side,
And see the span in between as too broken and wide,
and the distance they view as uncrossable space,
We can hope this bridge too will be mended by grace.

If we live long enough, almost everything we see, hear or do becomes a trigger for a memory of something we have seen, heard or done. It would be nice if we could do a selective match and everything we experience today would bring back only the best of yesterday, but our memories are not that easily parceled, and we're left to sort in the present the things of the past. What a gift. Each time we experience something painful or something joyful, we get another opportunity to put our past into a widening perspective.

This morning was exceptionally bright and beautiful, no clouds and little wind to stir the briskness of the winter chill. Standing at the pump, filling the car with gas, I was distracted by a tiny wave and a big grin. A little boy -- about four -- was perched like a cowboy on the side of the bed of a sleek Ford F-150 and he was delighted, freed from the confining car seat while his mother pumped gas and occasionally poked him in the ribs and ran her hand across his head. He laughed and kicked his boots against the side of the truck, leaning away from her, pretending to fend off her affections. And then he stopped, caught my eye, smiled, waved, and threw his hands up in the air with a "whatever" look to the sky.

Another car pulled up to the pump across from the truck and he repeated his act, a friend to all. His mother finished filling the truck, mouthed what looked like the words, "little monkey," swept him inside, buckled him up and away they drove.

Memories encroached. Me as a child . . . me as a father with little children . . . me as a grandfather. Generational moments of the decades . . . wide-eyed, bleary-eyed, wide-eyed again . . . sometimes teary-eyed with sadness, sometimes closed-eyed in frustration and regret, sometimes clear-eyed and brilliant blue in laughter or peace. The mind's eye fights the reluctant mind in the memory process, but very few things are sifted out. I wish I could say that all I see in the mental rear-view mirror is good, but it is not. Some of those bridges were tough to cross then and rough to remember now.

Though "bridges" serve only as metaphors in relation to our memories, it is amazing how many true bridges I can *remember*.

A bridge in the park near our home where my father would take us on visits. Made of large stones and mortar, it arched above a creek that often ran dry. We could have run across the ground but we always chose the bridge. I remember standing on it with my brother and my sisters while my dad took pictures of us with his black-and-white box camera. All was well on those too-infrequent Saturdays.

A bridge in the country near Bridgeport, Texas where my dad would stand with his 22 caliber rifle shooting beer bottles on the banks of the muddy river, occasionally picking off a wayward and clueless squirrel. The shots would echo through the countryside then and through my memory now.

A bridge near Denton, Texas where I posed for photos once, with long hair and a confident grin, looking for all the world like I had the world under control . . . shortly before my first fall as a college freshman, beginning a spiral into same-sex exploration that would have all my world under its temptation-fueled control for way too long and at too great a price.

There were more bridges, big and small, architectural wonders over great gorges to two-by-fours over grimy creek-beds. Too many to remember. Ahhh . . . see, some bridges just "burn" on their own.

The person trying to leave behind a regrettable past or overcome a suffocating present shrouded by sexual brokenness, whether unwanted same-sex attraction, pornography addiction, adultery or other, yearns for a sledgehammer to knock down those bridges, or fuel for a raging fire, plus the determination never to re-build or re-trace the steps across the perilous threatening plunge that remains beneath those beckoning bridges. Burn those bridges . . . one-by-one . . . crisp and done, like tossing photos in a campfire.

Memories, however, are not ashes. They don't follow the wind out onto the horizon and disappear into the night sky. They linger like a determined fog and hold us back for one more try above the gorge, reaching for what seem like irretrievable relationships with friends and family who may have long-since stopped waving and wondering. The toll booth on those bridges requires a second-or-more-chance ticket, but . . . that ticket may have burned with the bridge.

So, the question is, when one is determined to move on to a new life, how much energy should go into dismantling the stones and mortar, beams and planks, steel and lumber from the past? Maybe there are *good* reasons to return? In reality, each of our lives is a messy mixture of good and bad things seen, heard and done. The raging torch does not discriminate between Redwoods and scrub brush, the really good and the really bad; it burns it all if left to run its course.

If every bridge is burned, we become islands of ourselves. No thanks.

Some bridges smolder and remain unsafe for any further travel. People in your past who were a part of your sexual fall should remain in your past, left alone like hot coals. Intruding memories alone will be tough enough to take to God on a regular basis. Given time and left untended, those bridges will collapse on their own. Leave them to their own weight and don't try to convince yourself that you need to go back and make things right. That's what confession and prayer are for.

Some bridges were burned by others the minute we stepped off of them. We turn timidly around and nothing remains, not even a firm bank on which to start the rebuilding process. Running in the air like a hapless cartoon character, we eventually see there is nothing beneath our feet. If those who burned them ever relinquish control, perhaps God can rebuild those. For instance, while I am convinced God is hearing the prayers of many, most of my sons and my daughter have, at this point, moved even beyond waving distance. I've consumed a mountain of materials in my efforts to re-build that bridge and not even a rope extends across the chasm. This one is God's; His will to prevail.

Some bridges are just no longer bridges, no matter how hard you try to keep them spanning. Time takes care of some of them, but not if you refuse to cooperate. The man who abused me is, in all likelihood, dead, but, if not, the decades of distance makes him so to me. My father, who surrendered to alcohol, is also dead. Those of us who so long for the extension of forgiveness and grace for the harm we've done to others only pay lip service to those great gifts if we do not extend that grace and forgiveness to those who hurt us. One of the saddest sounds I hear are the plaintive cries of those still bound by past hurts done to them, allowing their present to be dominated by the pain of the past, clinging to it, claiming it as an identity.

"But, I can't move on," they say. "Too much happened to me for too long."

Buddy . . . that bridge needs to be burned. Crossing back and forth on it in your solo journey gets you nowhere. It's all beginning-agains and do-overs. Set fire to that one and you may soon see it is constructed only of memory. There's nothing real there anymore. As painful as it is to realize, the perpetrator likely moved on across that bridge. Unless there is something you can still do to protect others, let God collect that toll while you move on to the next bridge, and find that . . .

Some bridges are still beautiful and strong, like the people who stand upon them. Maybe you are afraid to take a step onto a bridge you only thought was burned, fearful it might collapse beneath the weight of history, succumbing to the reality of repeated failures. You don't trust it because you yourself seem so unworthy of trust. And yet, standing there in the middle of the bridge is someone who says "try again." A bridge-keeper, appointed by God Himself, who does not give up on you and will stand with you until your balance returns. A bridge-keeper positioned to prove not all bridges are burned.

Life is too precious to decide at some point that it is pointless to relentlessly pursue restoration. We're not bound by the bridges of the past when we are bound to the Ultimate Bridge-Builder. Only if we do not believe in God can we be excused from seeking to be renewed and restored to the persons He purposed us to be. We're not accidental tourists in a wayward world; we were planned and placed on a path . . . but found ourselves too enticed by a bridge to another direction.

And the God of all grace, who called you to His eternal glory in Christ, after you have suffered a little while, will Himself restore you and make you strong, firm and steadfast. -- 1 Peter 5:10

Even as Christians, we are not promised that we will be spared suffering and difficulty. In fact, the opposite is true. We *know* we will have difficulties. What God promises is that He will always restore us after any trial we undergo. Suffering is for a "little while" only, and will be followed by God's healing.

God's healing.

Now that's a bridge we need to cross when we come to it.

CHAPTER 18

IT REALLY WILL BE ALL RIGHT

Breathe deep . . .
Turn around . . .
Slow the mind . . .
Still the tongue . . .
Seek the eyes . . .
Extend the hand . . .
Feel the peace . . .
Take the love . . .
Breathe again.
Reconciliation.

I'm not sure who first said the words "divide and conquer,"
but I think I heard the devil cackling in the background. Through
the years, I have seen and felt how strife and anger and suspicion
and ignorance can be wielded like swords to separate and silence,
divide and conquer, substitute stilting shadows for life-giving
sunlight, bring down dark curtains between those who were
meant to love each other and lift each other up. Instead, turning
away, they withdraw from both sides and wander away once-
again bloodied . . . divided. Conquered, each. No winners here,
though one or the other declares a hollow victory, bolstered by
claims of greater goodness.

The result? Timidity on the part of one. Disturbing
determination from the other. Reaching out for reconciliation
dissolves into claims of manipulation, a rapid-fire repetition of
past failures, a painful presentation of the list of wrongs and the

ensuing self-defensiveness, hands flailing, voices rising, fingers accusing, backs turning. Walls thicken, hopes fade, chances of healing the rift recede. It will take more than a double-dog dare to bring either to the table again.

Why do we so lavishly award the devil what he thinks is his due?

"I know myself," we think. "I'll just screw this up anyway. I'm not trying again."

No you don't. You might not. Maybe you should; maybe you shouldn't.

"They know me," we think. "They're just waiting for me to screw this up."

No they don't. Maybe they are; maybe they aren't.

Maybe we think too much.

Perhaps it is easier to erect a wall of mirrors and see only ourselves, every flaw there to mock us in multiples, our own reflections crowding out the incrimination of others.

Easy or not, it isn't the right thing to do.

Breathe.

For the sexually-broken, relationships are decidedly complicated. It is not easy to walk through life balancing between the weight of judgment and the weight of want, pits on each side of the narrow path. The weariness of willful sinning that comes out of a will worn down by weakness pulls like quicksand, draining the energy needed to resist and stand on stable land. When your hand goes out and your cry is heard, but you grasp air and the response is silence, you are tempted to narrow your focus down to survival, just getting out of this pit and worrying about the others to come later. That's not progress. That's repetitive pain.

Being sexually-broken, with a past prone to bad decisions, does not determine that we are now devoid of discernment. If anything, we should be even more determined to make good decisions, especially about relationships. The truth of the matter is that some people may never be helpful in our struggle to re-establish a life that bears a resemblance to purity. Even some of the well-meaning are not well-equipped. It's not selfish to realize that we are the ones at risk here. Yes, others have been hurt by our failings and deserve to taste of the fruits of our repentance, and we have much making-up to do, but there will never be fruit if we are so distracted to please them, to perform, to perfect ourselves to their specifications. The road to professed perfection is paved with a preponderance of lies.

The devil would like little more than to keep the sexually-broken person in a round-robin of rejection, remorse and rebuilding. That's not repentance. It's self-torture and it demeans the good of those who really are pulling for you. Not the finger-pointers, but the ones who stand with palm extended and ankles braced against the edge, urging you to move out, not dig down deeper.

We *can* rebuild some relationships and build new and healthy ones. We just have to be willing to let some stones rest by the side in hopes that God will add them back to the wall in His due time. The devil would have us scramble around trying to put it all back together again, not wanting us to see the truth that many times God intends the new structure to be something altogether different.

So, how do we go about this rebuilding?

1. Distance yourself from strife. I don't know how many times -- although I am sure someone is probably keeping count -- I have prematurely approached someone who has declared themselves permanently separated from me -- and what they have declared as my overwhelming sinfulness -- and tried to get them to see me in a new light. I have learned now that if that darkness is to be penetrated, it will be by God, not me. Sometimes moving on is the only way to reduce the distance.

2. Don't give up the most important right of all. You have a right that cannot be stripped from you through any incrimination. In God's eyes, through the saving blood of Jesus Christ, you stand on equal footing with your accusers.

Yet to all who did receive Him, to those who believed in His name, He gave the right to become children of God -- children born not of natural descent, nor of human decision or a husband's will, but born of God.
-- John 1:12-13

You are one of God's children, by . . . right. And, if you are not, because you have not believed, you will be if you do.

3. Don't ever allow yourself to think that God loves you any less than He loves anyone else. Sometimes it can be difficult to realize the great immensity of His love against the diminished love of those who have been deceived or damaged by our brokenness. That pesky question . . . *"How can God love a sinner like me?"* . . . was answered long, long ago. He loves you. Don't doubt that. Use it for the power it bears in your life on the days you feel unlovely or unloved. It does not wane.

4. Wesist the wedgemaster. Run like a wascally wabbit when the devil descends to drive wedges between you and those who are still able to care. Haven't we already given the devil enough reasons to delight over his destructiveness without letting him devastate us more by dealing a death-blow to our dealings with those who have been gifted by God to love us? I find it hard to accept love, and yet . . . God *is* love.

Submit yourselves, then, to God. Resist the devil, and he will flee from you. Come near to God and He will come near to you. Wash your hands, you sinners, and purify your hearts, you double-minded. -- James 4:7-8

5. Be tender; be receptive. Repetitive remorse can lead to flinching, a weariness that trying again is just a part of failing again. We walk as if we are bruised; don't touch. Don't talk to me. And yet, it is often a touch, a word that soothes and heals. And it is through the hands and hearts of those around us that God will have His work done within us. Receive from those He has chosen to use in your life.

A bruised reed He will not break, and a smoldering wick He will not snuff out. -- Isaiah 42:3

6. Do it all again if you have to. Distance yourself from strife . . . remember your right to be a child of God . . . realize His enduring love for you . . . resist the devil . . . be receptive to God's work through others. These good things do not change.

> Breathe deep . . .
> Turn around . . .
> Slow the mind . . .
> Still the tongue . . .
> Seek the eyes . . .
> Extend the hand . . .
> Feel the peace . . .
> Take the love . . .
> Breathe again.

> It really wiil be all right.

CHAPTER 19

IF YOU'RE HEALING
AND YOU KNOW IT . . .

It is often in the small things that we feel pain. A paper cut.
A sticker on a barefoot heel. A stubbed toe. A hangnail.
An empty mailbox.
A silent phone.
A leaf drifting to the lawn in a season of change.
A slow-fading photo.
A sigh.
A looking away.
A turn.
A train in the distance.
A secret.
A reflection in a mirror.
A splinter.
A memory.
This is not to downplay the greater pain of a car wreck or a
tumble down the stairs . . . or the death of someone you love.
Broken bones and broken hearts. In these times, though,
emergency crews or skilled physicians or grief counselors come to
your aid and pull you through and put you back together, set you
upright again and give you a nudge to move you on.
It takes time to heal.
I remember when I was a little boy dressed only in a pair
of shorts, running free with abandon, until I tumbled down a hill

into a thick growth of wild blackberry bushes. Some of the thorns punched into me and others just left tracks on my skin as I passed through them. A hidden rock made contact with my knee and gashed it open. I was frozen in the pain of the fall and when I stood and looked around, there was no one there to call on . . . and the only way out of the patch was to cross back through it, picking a path to avoid as many thorns as possible. Once home, I soaked in the bathtub and the water took on a pinkish tinge from the tiny wounds. For days I was fascinated with the scab on my knee, which stood out like a small island, but slowly shrunk and then vanished beneath the new skin.

I healed. '

I remember driving my convertible to Galveston after my freshman year in college. . . around and around Galveston . . . and all the way down the coast to Louisiana and back to Dallas with the top down under the summer sun. I abandoned my shirt and all common sense. My face, my shoulders, my chest, my arms, and the tops of my legs were as red as a ripe tomato. Touch me and we both die. Blisters rose; skin peeled.

I healed.

A couple of years ago I had a fairly significant surgery leaving about an 8-inch gash through the mid-section, all stapled shut neatly. Within hours after the surgery, the nurses were getting me out of bed to walk the halls, wincing with every step. Sneezes would send me into painful spasms; bending in the middle to pull myself out of my recovery recliner in the living room felt like I was re-tearing everything. A few weeks after the surgery, I returned to the doctor's office to face a cheery nurse who pulled out a tool that looked like something I neglect in the garage. "This is going to hurt, so we may as well get after it and get 'er done," she said, about the time she pulled the first staple.

I healed.

As we travel through life, we tumble into thorny bushes when we're not paying attention to where we're headed as we explore. Seeking fun and pleasure, we can shrivel in the sun when we forget to seek the protection of the shade. And sometimes we just get cut wide open and find ourselves immobilized.

You can heal. Whether your brokenness is an addiction to pornography, a lust that has driven you into adultery, or a gnawing temptation that wears you down and pulls you into the sin of homosexuality, masquerading as a balm of acceptance for the gaping wound of rejection. You can heal, but you have to pull yourself up and out of the recliner first. And you may have to expose the scar to the light.

With apologies to the Latvian folk singer who wrote the original happy song:

If you're healing and you know it, clap your hands
If you're healing and you know it, then you really ought to show it.
If you're healing and you know it, clap your hands.

Our post-fall life is not limited to lamentations. God is not like the doctor who pats your leg as he sits beside your bed and solemnly says: "There's nothing more we can do." God is never outdone by the disorder of our lives. When we cry out for healing, we can hear "yes," from God if we are willing to say "no" to the world and the paralysis of brokenness. And then get up and walk.

Jesus knew what they were thinking and asked, "Why are you thinking these things in your hearts? Which is easier: to say, 'Your sins are forgiven,' or to say, 'Get up and walk'? But I want you to know that the Son of Man has authority on earth to forgive sins." So He said to the paralyzed man, "I tell you, get up, take your mat and go home." Immediately he stood up in front of them, took what he had been lying on and went home praising God. -- Luke 5:22-25

Walk without fear. -- First of all, you cannot heal for others' sake, so resist that temptation. This is truly a point in life where "For God's sake" makes complete sense. I tried healing for my children's sake, for the church's sake, for pity's sake . . . and certainly for my wife's sake. That type of healing leads too easily to hiding; to projecting an image of well-being that makes everyone else feel better, but actually casts a shadow of deceit. Determined as that type of healing may be, it depends on you way too much and on Christ way too little. He was never about

100

pretense; if He said someone was healed, He meant it. They got up; they moved on. Exchange the pain of falling with the pain of rehab, and stop worrying about whether people will believe you or accept you. Some will; others won't. Some may never come back; others may come in. If your healing depends on anyone or anything beyond Christ, you may never get to pull the staples.

Walk with hope. -- The sexually-broken, in the pursuit of wholeness, often spend too much time counting time, marking the hours, then the days, then the months, recording the passage to the inevitable fall and the beginning of another count. How is this helpful? How is it hopeful? I understand the encouragement of a record of sobriety, whether from lust, alcohol or cupcakes. But, just as we should not keep a record of wrongs, we need to be careful how we keep our record of rights. If we are so focused on making it through this day, we lose focus of where we're headed in our freedom and we slow the pace, chopping it into minor victories, while ignoring the goal of the greater battle to live in constant hope, born of redemption. Fear builds in the absence of hope. While we need be constantly on guard, we won't walk far if we fear there's a bear around every corner.

Walk without defense. -- If we can do all things through Christ because He gives us strength, then that clearly means we cannot do all things without Him because we lack the strength He gives. That includes defending a past He washes away; explaining the fading stain of dirt He's washing away. The countless conversations and the endless e-mails, the explanations and justifications, the reasons and the excuses, the repeated apologies and appeals for forgiveness are like nervous little dogs nipping at your heels as you seek to walk free. Not dangerous, but very annoying and never satisfied with the pace. Let Christ be your defense as you live your life to please God. He can reveal it to others in a way you cannot because He does not bear the stain of deceit. Yes, we need to ask for forgiveness from those we have hurt and we need to repair what we have destroyed, but, when the "Why?" becomes overbearing, drop the burden of defense and fall on the sword of grace, and hope for mercy.

Pain pursues us, but mercy renews us. Hurt lurks; grace reveals.

101

As you feel your way to freedom, which may seem like uncharted territory, there is only one dependable guide. Christ alone heals the soul.

I walked into a 7-Eleven the other day and came face-to-face with Randy, a leader from a church I attended when my sexual sin was revealed, a church which removed me through the exercise of church discipline. Randy had signed the letter that let me know. The years have passed and there we stood, only a few feet apart, but distanced greatly by past words and present mistrust. It was an expressionless encounter. No "how are you?" No "have a good day." No smile, in fact, and the brief acknowledgement of presence quickly masked by both of us. Not that long ago, that brief encounter would have left a lasting pain and would have prompted me to want to do something about it. State my case. Demand forgiveness. Not this time. I left with my caffeine fix and my peace.

I am healing.

Heal. Set aside your fear. Show the presence of hope. Drop the defense. Take up your mat. Go home.

Pull the staples.

CHAPTER 20

FOR THE THINGS WE CAN'T ERASE

"Out, damn'd spot! Out, I say!"
-- Lady Macbeth, from Shakespeare's *Macbeth*

I wish -- though I don't believe in wishes -- that I could take a number two pencil and write down on a blue-lined piece of three-hole-punched notebook paper the moments of my life, label it "draft," study it a bit, and then turn the pencil around to the pink side -- the eraser -- and smudge away forever a line here and there . . . many lines, major smudges. Study it a bit more, swipe away with my hand the little black rubber crumbles, dirty from the mix of pink eraser and pencil lead, onto the floor . . . gone. Erased.

I would take a deep breath, sit back and sigh, copy the remains onto a fresh piece of paper, smooth it out and turn it in . . . to someone. The only copy. Not a draft, but an A-deserving masterpiece. In ink now, my finest handwriting, nothing to erase; no need. I would crumple up the old messy draft, toss it away with no further thought, done, rise, walk.

I wish . . . though I don't believe in wishes.

"Free will" is more like a Sharpie than a number-two pencil. The use of it leaves permanent marks . . . and often results in a lot of crumbling-up and tossing and shredding instead of erasing. Out, damn'd spot. A part of me would much prefer the sweet smell of a new pink eraser over the black acrid smell of a inky black marker leaving trails and tracks that reflect the staggering stumbles of the exercise of my free will. Can't erase?

Reach for the White-Out, which will leave a pasty crumbly mess itself, no match for the thick black markings of me being me . . . showing through.

What would I erase?

Selfishness.

Self-pity.

Self-defensiveness.

Self-gratification.

Okay . . . well, maybe that's a little too much "self."

How about . . .

Deception?

Fear?

Doubt?

Weakness?

Self-reliance? Oops . . . there's that "self" thing again.

What would *you* erase?

Maybe it would be better to just gently smudge out a moment in time, here and there. Problem is, some of them are so darkly there that the only way to get them out is to rub all the way through the paper, leaving a hole that speaks as clearly as the original deed itself. I've tried. Accepting the fact that I can't erase the deeds of others, I settled for the hope that I could erase my responses to them. Kind of like when you have a long word problem on a math quiz that leaves you stymied and you try this and that . . . erase . . . try again . . . erase. The word problem is still there no matter what you do to the answer.

I wish -- though I don't believe in wishes -- that I could erase the moment that I leaned over to the rolled-down window of a little beige Volkswagen on a foggy campus night in college and accepted a ride out of the drizzle. I would have erased the route to his house and the memory of having been there. Indelible ink.

I would erase the first lie I told. No, not some silly little lie about taking a cookie before dinner, but the first lie I told myself: "this doesn't really matter. I'm not hurting anyone anyway." When you fall for that lie and carry it around inside for a while and find that you can fool yourself into believing it, you start trying it out on others to see if they might fall for it too. Pretty soon, it's you, not a lie. Deception.

If I could not erase the lie, then maybe I could erase the pain that grew from it? The wondering of others pondering the inconsistencies that characterized my character. I became the word problem for which there were no answers and, once they had unsuccessfully figured on it long enough to leave a hole in the page of my life, the hole remains.

I would erase the times I tried to deflect the truth of my actions by pointing a finger at someone else, even if . . . no, I'm not going to make any justifications now because that would only leave me with more I would want to erase. Like the time my son confronted me with knowledge he had that I had sinned sexually and I defended myself by pointing a finger at the *way* he was confronting me with an anger that was totally justified by my mis-behavior and his hurt, disappointment and disgust. As lies do, it made things worse.

After owning up to true accusations by erasing deception . . . I would then erase the moment I failed to act forcefully enough on a false accusation made against me and let my shame and guilt from true things allow false ones to go unanswered, adding layers of thickness and cubits of height to a wall that now seems impenetrable and unclimbable because of a lie, or, more politely put, a false accusation. I've learned now that anytime a false accusation stands, truth suffers and when truth suffers, we all do.

I would erase the times I said "I will not fail again." I know the devil smiled at that one, for though he could not have known for sure that I would fail again, my claims of strength must have redoubled his efforts. How he must love the little word "I." How he must rejoice (does the devil rejoice?) at the longer word "again," when it is part of a vow, no matter how intentionally intended. "I" would smudge out the word "I" and try never to write it again with the word "will." God wills.

I would erase the times I hid my unpleasantness behind my efforts to please. The times I worked harder on looking good than on being good, on doing right instead of being right, on projecting an image instead of revealing a reality.

I would erase the haughtiness with which I approached the earliest offers of help and I would scribble in a "yes . . . I need help," and write in clearest cursive, "thank you."

But instead of an eraser, I have pages and pages of permanent words representing my life ranging from deception to desperation, from putrid prose to pure poetry, from painful falling to joyful soaring, from self . . . there I go again . . . reviling to self-restoring, from quiet hiding to loud revealing, from darkness and heaviness to light and . . . lightness. All there, like a jumble with words out of place, a sentence for which no blackboard is large enough on which to diagram to anyone's specifications. (Like that very sentence.)

I've looked at life from both sides now
From up and down and still somehow
It's life's illusions I recall
I really don't know life at all.
-- Joni Mitchell

Count the "I"s in the lyrics. No wonder we fall so easily to the illusion of life instead of the truth of it. Or at least, "I" do . . . or did. And when we do, we yearn for the eraser as a quick answer to the question, "Why did I do that?" And we walk around in a stupor, wringing our hands and muttering madly, like Lady Macbeth, or woefully taking the stage like Joni and blaming our actions on our inability to get a grasp on . . . life.

. . . I came that they may have life, and have it abundantly. -- John 10:10

That's the "I" that really matters and the life that is no illusion.

There is no eraser, but there is unlimited chalkboard space. Scribble like Einstein to fit your life into a legalism that will fill every inch of writable room and still leave you unfulfilled and scrambling to do more to say more and be more and prove more, or accept that you will never make it without one word: grace.

For of His fullness we have all received, and grace upon grace. For the Law was given through Moses; grace and truth were realized through Jesus Christ. -- John 1:16-17

For the things we can't erase . . . there's grace.

CHAPTER 21

TO ME OR NOT TO ME?

We were once, all us, little me's, front and center on the merry-go-round, which can become a fitting metaphor for our lives. Round and round we go; where we'll end up, nobody knows. For too long for me, it depended on who was pushing and how hard. Just keep smiling and whirling . . . until you fall off. In our early days, someone picks us up and stretches a band-aid across our wounded knee and offers us a Popsicle and tells us to hang-on better and go a little slower. In later days, they point and whisper and you are but a silly fool who should have known better than to go on the ride in the first place. The pain of the fall does not diminish with the passage of time, but as the dirt becomes more familiar you lay there longer until you realize that at some point you are expected to get up on your own.

I'm not a potter and I don't have a way with clay, but if I was and if I did, I would certainly have gone a little lighter on my ears . . . and maybe shaved a bit off the high level of uncertainty and doubt, added a bit of reinforcement to the walls for resistance to sin, and certainly upped the awareness to yield and the desire to seek. A little reshaping within and without: a better vessel. Instead, the designer ears are there, the doubt is clearly visible in the color of the clay and the edges have become brittle and vulnerable through the effects of sin, the pouring spout itself a bit eroded from the corrosion of bitterness.

It's me. Slowly-changing, yet ever-resembling the me I have always been. The old me cast aside to become new, but always tip-tapping at the window panes, begging to come back inside, the old eyes peering into the new, questioning and accusing and sowing confusion. The where I've been challenging the where I'm headed. The I'm free of me mocking the me who's free.

Who would have thought that a little "me" could be so enveloping, so demanding, so revealing, so undoing, so pursuing, so unforgiving, so deceiving, so unworthy, so treacherous and sly, so bound?

Me.

Who would have thought that a little "me" could be so beautiful, so valuable, so intricate, so unique, so sought, so true, so worthy, so accepting and open, so free?

Me.

Sometimes I think the principalities of darkness have nothing on the internal struggle between me and me. And then I realize it is not me, but the proximity of those principalities and the propensity I have to welcome or to at least justify their presence, proclaiming myself too weak to push back against them. After all, I am just . . . me.

I think when we are unhappy with "me," two things happen. We try harder to be like others and we try harder to hide the me we don't really want to be. In doing so, we sometimes pick up characteristics and traits that were never ours in the first place and we hide others that we might have just been misusing or neglecting somehow, which become rusty and misplaced, but were a big part of the "we," that's you and me. We self-diagnose and we react with reinvention to the diagnoses offered by others and hop on the "maybe-this-will-work" merry-go-round and spin the days away until we hit the dirt in an out-of-balance daze that reveals to everyone we are just "me" trying to be what others wish we were. You can travel a long ways down the right road in this life and them stumble on an errant stone and be declared a treacherous transient by the righteous who move to the other side and continue on their way, leaving an unfolded map at your feet, just in case you wake up and want to join them on a perfect journey.

It seems like we think preservation comes through complication. The more difficult we can make this path to change, the more we will prove we deserve to have arrived. The more of "me" we can leave behind, the more different we can become, the more we deserve for others to embrace "the new me." The more others can spell it out in as big a word as possible, the more they can measure your success against their own.

It doesn't really work that way. The me I am today is so different than the me I was just a few short years back, but yet I am the me I have always been. Confounding as that may be to others, that's how ·God works. He creates a "me," loves a "me," frees a "me," forgives a "me," hears a "me," wants a "me." He changes me, but he still knows me as the me He created me to be.

Unfortunately, that's not how we work, so caught up are we in "change me," that we cringe at the idea that we are, despite our dings, still created in His image, still worthy of His love, still forgiven, still able to be softened and shaped and molded to conform to His likeness instead of to the world's, which, in truth doesn't so much care about you or me . . . but only about what they can do about us to make us more what they want us to be, depending on the perspective of the "me" they themselves happen to be.

And since we want them to be happy with who we are, we bend and twist and project our recovery and rejoice in our victory and smother our misery at the encumbrances of change. If we can provide enough positive evidence, they'll be pleased. You've probably already tried to please men, becoming what you thought would make you more wanted so you could have more of what you thought *you* wanted. How has that worked out for you? It didn't do a lot for me.

On the rebound-merry-go-round, such a pattern produces a warped repentance, a check-list once again designed to please men, a facade rather than a changed heart. Just wait and see . . . I'm a brand new me. And then, if the repentance is not real, under the pressure of time and temptation, the facade crumbles and the burdens win and we retreat into the same old me-ness.

"Come to Me, all you who are weary and burdened, and I will give you rest. -- Matthew 11:28

While we are caught up in "woe is me," He says "come to Me."

Then He said to them all: "Whoever wants to be My disciple must deny themselves and take up their cross daily and follow Me." -- Luke 9:23

While we are caught up in finding ourselves He says "follow Me."

You know what really stands out to me in those verses? The word "me." Jesus was clearly comfortable with "being me."

And so should we be.

The me is not the problem. It's the "my." It's the things we bring in and make ours. It's what we do and allow to be done to the "me." From the moment we as little ones point and shout and cry out "me want!" to the moment we begin to point inwardly and cry silently "want me?" we are confusing "my" and "me." My body -- ears and all -- is not me. My possessions are not me. My cravings are not me. My sins are not me.

I am me. Heart and soul. Created in the image. All that is within me is me . . . and He is in me. All those other things that swirl around me and label me? They may be what people see, but they're not me. But, as long as I believe they are, they *will* define me. As long as I let others say that what they think of me really is me, then my reactions will determine where I go and what I do and how I live and who I serve and who I please and who I seek and who I need and what I want.

We lay out a plan to help us find freedom, yet we know He set us free.

We strive mightily to find peace though He clearly says He will just give it to us.

We look for love though He says He has always loved us.

We bargain for acceptance though He says He will never leave us.

We pine for our place in life though He has already prepared a place for us beyond it.

We walk stooped over in shame and stumbling under guilt, though He says He forgives us.

If we believe what He says, we can certainly reduce the stress of striving, looking, bargaining, pining, stopping, stumbling. It would definitely leave true energy for real repentance.

Which begs the question. What in the world is wrong with me? Just that. The world. It's nothing that Christ can't handle when the me of you becomes we in Him.

Sound too easy? That's what the world -- caught up in the do it my way way -- wants you to think. Which brings us back to "my."

Me . . . or Christ in me? That is the question.

CHAPTER 22

BUILDING A BRIDGE
OUT OF BROKENNESS

"I cannot stress this enough to you, but I'll still say it: I'll never be Christian. I think your Bible is nothing more than a piece of literature. I don't believe in your God, and never will. But I will criticize you when you use your God to "fix" homosexuality, as if it were something to be fixed."
-- *An anonymous young friend*

"Broken does not seem like something Jesus would want us to say."
-- *Comment in on-line Christian Group*

When you raise five children, you hear the words "It's broken" way too often. Favorite toys, birds' wings, Christmas ornaments, bats, even cars, are presented in their brokenness, sometimes with a shriek or sometimes with a shrug. Sometimes with a plea for a fix; sometimes with acceptance that it is time to move beyond . . . in hopes of something new and better. Sometimes a little glue or a Phillips screwdriver is enough to put things right again. But sometimes the reality is that if the bird can't fly, it will probably die. At some point, everything . . . everyone . . . will be broken.

I have broken only two bones in my lifetime. A wrist and a rib. The result of each was an increase in pain, a decrease in mobility and a denied sense of helplessness during a time of adjustment and healing. I still have the wrist and the rib and they both work just fine now.

I didn't *decide* to break my wrist. I didn't *plan* to break a rib. Absent of decisions or plans, they still broke. And the rest of me? It compensated, covered the effects of each break, rose to the occasion, took up the slack, pretended all was well.

I wasn't doing anything wrong, either time. The wrist, in fact, sacrificed itself in an effort to keep me from tumbling further on the hills and landscape rocks in our backyard as I was weed-eating in preparation for my daughter's birthday party. It backed up the efforts of the palm, which threw itself down in a sacrificial act of protection. Snap, crackle, pop . . . . swell up, stop bending and retreat on a wrist R&R.

In my stubbornness, it took me several hours to grasp that the hand extending from the wrist had no grasp. "I guess it's broken."

The rib? Talk about a bone with a mind of its own. It snapped in a concerted resistance effort against self-improvement. I was suspended between two weight benches, ankles on one, hands on the other, lifting myself up and down almost effortlessly (yeah . . .) when all of a sudden it felt as if my workout partner had amused himself by slamming my rib cage with a sledgehammer.

"Who did that?" I exclaimed, lowering myself to the floor between the benches.

The rib was silent . . . and everyone else just paused and resumed working out. Standing up was torture; breathing was like ingesting needles. My usual self-medication -- denial -- ran in with a rush of adrenaline and I said, as I would do if run over by a road-grader: "I'm fine."

In about six weeks, I could say "I'm fine" with a straight face, not a grimace of pain.

I guess it really was broken.

Brokenness is usually pretty obvious. A wrist that won't bend; a rib that feels like a blade in your lungs. A bulb that shines no light and spreads itself in shards. A tree limb laying in the yard. A glass in pieces on a hard tile floor. The solutions are usually obvious too: screw in a new bulb; fetch the ax; sweep the floor. The light is back; the branch is firewood; your bare feet are safe. We respond and tidy up and move on.

But what about sexual brokenness?

Well . . . we tend to respond . . . tidy up . . . and move on. The response can be a muted "oh" or a shocked "Oh . . . my God!" Tidying up ranges from a-pat-on-the-back-and-a-passing-prayer to a dictatorial list of dos-and-don'ts delivered by a spiritual watchdog dutifully recording progress on a report card, marking pass or fail. Moving on can be as beautiful as a bless you and an arm around the shoulder as we go together . . . or a disdaining look of disturbed incredulity that becomes a never-knew-you-never-will insistence in denial, a multi-directional scattering to put as much distance between thee and me as possible.

We be movin' on . . . us . . . the unbroken. Or at least, the undiscovered, for brokenness is not limited to sexuality. Indeed, would not denial of brokenness be brokenness?

Adios . . . *amigos?*

There are those who hang close and respond with what they hope will be comforting words: *"you'll be fine."* Is that somehow expected to be more comforting than our own well-worn, oft-mis-proved *"I'll be fine?"* Trite answers are convenient, and can even sound reassuring, but they're not compassionate. How about a more honest one: "Yes, you are broken. Like me. But you don't have to be. Me either."

Fortunately for us, we're not a cold, indifferent piece of glass that slips off the edge of a counter and smashes into a million pieces, lacking even the wherewithal to ask for "a little help here, please?" We're not a tree limb looking dumbly up at the tree with an "I've fallen and I can't get up" plea. And we're not a spent bulb. We're a dimmer light, perhaps, than we want to be . . . but we are not without the opportunity to shine again.

Ahh brokenness . . . let me count the ways. Wondrously made we are, with many parts, in need of constant maintenance.

Are you a liar?

Do you gossip?

Do you have a heart of stone when you see the needs of others?

Do you lust?

Speak profanity?

Feast your senses on pornography?

Neglect the homeless?

Commit adultery?

114

Withhold forgiveness?

Are you greedy?

Have you turned your back on your mother and father . . . as in not honoring them?

Do you fill your mind with impure thoughts and reject Scripture?

Neglect to worship?

Feed your pride?

Boast a bit?

Yep . . . you're broken. Of course, if I recount your sins and ignore mine, that would certainly be a sign of . . . brokenness.

I learned, in writing an earlier book, *Surviving Sexual Brokenness: What Grace Can Do,* that some of the sexually-broken take offense at the term. Actually, I understand that. Some do not even see themselves as broken, but instead see their sexual expression – homosexuality, pornography, etc. – as a reflection of how God created them. This distinction is primarily one of faith. It's a choice: the Word or the world. If you have faith and you believe God, you know what His Word says about sexuality. If you go beyond that, you're broken and you probably know it. However, if you reject faith and believe what the *world* says about sexuality, then you probably believe you're not broken and are fairly sure of it. Well, actually, you really are broken, but if you have no faith, you *think* you're not, which can seem oddly comforting and permanently condemning. For people in that position, perhaps it is better that they not consider themselves broken, for the *world* will not repair them. Why?

It's broken.

The world's embrace will not chase away the chill of emptiness for the soul who seeks through faith to be what God intended: whole.

God gave us "*The* Word," but we have come up with so many more. We live in interpretive-Babel, never sure in the first place that people mean what they say or even know what they are saying means. So, brokenness -- an acknowledgement that we need God's healing -- becomes instead synonymous with no-goodness, and when we hear it spoken of us by others, we see the broom sweeping up the shattered glass for the trash. How dare you? I'm not *that* broken.

I am broken. Thank God. The result has been an increase in pain, a decrease in mobility and a denied sense of helplessness during a time of adjustment and healing. Not so different than the twisted wrist and the fractured rib. No one could really see those either. On the day I broke the wrist, I made it all the way through my daughter's party without saying a word. On the day I cracked the rib, I finished the workout. We compensate for our brokenness until we cannot bear the pain or we cannot walk the walk of wholeness.

But God restores, repairs, redeems and returns me to the shelf. He uses me. Out of my brokenness, He builds something new.

But . . . *SEXUAL* brokenness? That sounds more like something just doesn't work, for which there are countless remedies and prescriptions. Or have you not watched television or opened your spam e-mail?

What is sexual brokenness? It is any expression of sexuality that is not what God intended. After all, remember, He looked at everything He had made and said "it was good." The path from the garden was clearly a steady decline, swiftly descending from uncomfortable nakedness to homosexuality, pornography, heterosexual sexual addiction, lust, adultery, idolatry . . . and more. That's brokenness. That's sin. And it is not good.

Maybe we don't like the brokenness terminology because we're so accustomed to discarding broken things. In the spring time, if you drive through the neighborhoods, you see cabinets and bookshelves and chairs and lamps and TVs, perched along the curb with signs: "take me," or "free." Why? Usually because they're broken. Someone picks them up and fixes them and they live on in their inanimate way.

But that's the world. The world eventually discards everything.

In God's view, brokenness is hopefulness. A broken heart, for instance, is the centerpiece for healing. Hearts are made brand new. A broken spirit soars to greater strength when healed. It is in our brokenness that we turn to Him and He responds.

My sacrifice, O God, is a broken spirit; a broken and contrite heart You,
God, will not despise. -- Psalm 51:17

So, make a sacrifice. Certainly give God your best . . . and certainly give God your brokenness. He knows what it is; He knows what it means; He knows what it's costing you; He knows what to do. He knows you.

So . . . would He – Jesus – or would He not tell someone they were broken?

I believe He would, but only because He knew they were on the verge of wholeness, the objective of everyone who knows Christ. He didn't go around pointing out brokenness and leaving people bewildered in peace-less pieces. He made them whole.

God, in His kindness, reveals to us our brokenness, which brings to us our tears of repentance, which drop to soften the hardened soil of our life in which He plants his new seeds and healing grows.

And therein is a bridge . . . out of brokenness.

Brokenness, blessedness, bridges. They all begin with "B."

ENCOURAGING WORDS OF HOPE

CONSIDER HIDING THESE VERSES IN YOUR HEART

But your iniquities have separated you from your God; your sins have hidden His face from you, so that He will not hear. -- Isaiah 59:2

Be strong and courageous. Do not be afraid or terrified because of them, for the Lord your God goes with you; He will never leave you nor forsake you. -- Deuteronomy 31:6

For I am convinced that neither death nor life, neither angels nor demons, neither the present nor the future, nor any powers, neither height nor depth, nor anything else in all creation, will be able to separate us from the love of God that is in Christ Jesus our Lord. -- Romans 8:38-40

Teach me your way, Lord; lead me in a straight path because of my oppressors. Do not turn me over to the desire of my foes, for false witnesses rise up against me, spouting malicious accusations. -- Psalm 27:11-12

And that is what some of you were. But you were washed, you were sanctified, you were justified in the name of the Lord Jesus Christ and by the Spirit of our God. -- 1 Corinthians 6:11

I lift up my eyes to the mountains -- where does my help come from? My help comes from the Lord, the Maker of heaven and earth. He will not let your foot slip -- He who watches over you will not slumber; -- Psalm 121:1-3

But the seed on good soil stands for those with a noble and good heart, who hear the word, retain it, and by persevering produce a crop. -- Luke 8:15

"For I know the plans I have for you," declares the Lord, "plans to prosper you and not to harm you, plans to give you hope and a future." -- Jeremiah 29:11

And the God of all grace, who called you to His eternal glory in Christ, after you have suffered a little while, will Himself restore you and make you strong, firm and steadfast. -- 1 Peter 5:10

Yet to all who did receive Him, to those who believed in His name, He gave the right to become children of God -- children born not of natural descent, nor of human decision or a husband's will, but born of God. -- John 1:12-13

Submit yourselves, then, to God. Resist the devil, and he will flee from you. Come near to God and He will come near to you. Wash your hands, you sinners, and purify your hearts, you double-minded. -- James 4:7-8

A bruised reed He will not break, and a smoldering wick He will not snuff out. -- Isaiah 42:3

. . . I came that they may have life, and have it abundantly. -- John 10:10

For of His fullness we have all received, and grace upon grace. For the Law was given through Moses; grace and truth were realized through Jesus Christ. -- John 1:16-17

Then He said to them all: "Whoever wants to be My disciple must deny themselves and take up their cross daily and follow Me. -- Luke 9:23

My sacrifice, O God, is a broken spirit; a broken and contrite heart You, God, will not despise. -- Psalm 51:17

FAITH

CHAPTER 23

WHO TOLD YOU YOU WERE NAKED?

One of the most discouraging aspects of battling a deeply-internalized sexual issue is that, even after you face it, fight it, and deprive it, something in that deep-internal goes right back to work to revive it. You choke it, pound it, bury it, surrender it, and then, before you know it, you're back under it. You toss it out the window on your journey to freedom and about the time you peek in the rear-view mirror, it's splatting on the windshield.

I've heard of -- and would like to shake the hand of -- some people who faced-down the addictive nature of sexual brokenness and, in that very moment, rose from that spot of confrontation, not momentarily cleansed and standing in the timidity of repentance, but forever unshackled and absent the pull of a perceived need and a nagging want. They stand tall and shout the call of freedom. They see trees like men walking and a light so brilliant the fog is now mere memory. I've heard their testimonies and reflected on the sovereignty of God to do that . . . for them . . . but it somehow made God seem so selective.

I've wondered in the past if it was just my lack of faith that left me sitting in the valley beside the mountain mouthing "move." Or was it an allergy to grace that left me avoiding the light of His forgiveness and restoration, opting instead for the darker recesses

of the depths of deception? Did I misunderstand mercy? Did I --
while railing at others for doing so -- view my sin as greater than
God's vision? Was I my own stingy keeper of the key to the door
of hope?

Are you?

I think sometimes we content ourselves -- though there is
no real contentedness to it at all -- with knowing that *we
know where* the door is, with knowing that *we can* knock, with
knowing *we have* a key, with knowing that *we can run* in that
direction if we really need to, with knowing that *we will find*, on
the other side, light and warmth and truth. And yet we go on,
comforting ourselves a bit by proximity, staying close enough to
the door, but keeping the key in our pocket like some insurance
policy, just in case we truly find out that all the lies of the world
really are just that. Lies.

In an odd twist of clever deception, the enemy makes the
things outside the door seem so tangible and immediate. We look
longingly at the door and believe the lies of the enemy we have
already -- through our endless u-turns -- surrendered to, forfeiting
the right to even finger the key, much less slide it into the lock
upon which we are so fixated. We're not good enough anymore
for His goodness. Too bad, so sad. Too late, your fate. And so we
comfort ourselves by pulling the darkness in around us and turn
away from the reality that He leaves the light on for us.

So . . . we wonder. Why doesn't He just throw open the
door and grab us as we slink away from the stoop? Pull us in,
slam the door behind us and bolt it. Never let us out again.

Oh sure . . . that sounds just like us, doesn't it? Demanding
God strip us of our freedom, take away our will, separate us
forcefully from the sin that so enthralls us. Just blind our eyes and
banish all temptation. Do we want Him to remove from us
everything that should drive us to Him and then naively think we
will be so gratified we will glorify Him forever even though we
would no longer need Him, having no need to despair and seek in
the absence of all confusion? You go, God. If You really want us to
be so pure and holy, then you do it, God. I know you can.

You do? You know He can?

Then why flee the door?

It's hard to know how sincere someone is about giving up if you don't know for sure how hard they fought against the giving in. I remember that beyond the original temptation was the great temptation to give up hope, accept fate, make the best of it, count my losses and look for some sort of justification that would allow me to escape the judgment of others and dismantle the complicated and conflicting self in a total embrace of sexuality, as if self-satisfaction was the answer to all the exasperation of life. It was especially tempting when, whacked by the tidal wave of my revealed sinfulness, my children walked away, my friends departed, my church folded exasperated arms against me, while, at the same time, culture chimed in with all the reasons I should rise beyond the ignorance and embrace the obvious: "being gay is about as good as it gets in this world." It's the domain of the creative and witty and intelligent, the self-actualized and contented ones, the ones who've discovered finally the meaning of loving oneself.

And, in the midst of loving themselves, they are also the sad and the lonely and the searching and the longing and the self-haters, always in pursuit of . . . something. After all, why would gays be deprived of the emotional and relational deficits everyone else suffers?

If we make our decisions on anything less than a full-flung pursuit of the truth, we should not be surprised to look up one day and see that the door from which we rarely strayed has become so distant that our eyes can barely see it and the key so deep within our pockets that our fingers barely reach it. But . . . the door and the key both are still there.

That's how truth is. It sails like an ever-free bird above the waves of culture, with the land always in sight. Truth doesn't bend beneath the beckoning call to change. Truth does not yield to counterfeited peacefulness. Truth does not cave into the ceaseless call to clarify truth itself. It is just truth. Unchanging, unwavering. Efforts to weaken it only serve to invite the inevitable emergence of the strength of truth.

When you find yourself signaling a left turn into another u-turn, heading back towards the places you wish you'd never been but for some reason long to re-visit . . . it's time to ponder truth. Here's a question you might want to ask yourself:

"Who told you you were naked?"

That's a follow-up question actually. God first asked Adam: "Where are you?" Then, when Adam explained that he had been hiding because he was naked, God said, "Who told you you were naked?"

It wasn't God.

If you have any doubt that the confusion and the sorrow and the anger and the fear and the frustration and the doubt that drive you to and away from the door are what God intended for you rather than what the world uses to ensnare you and enswhirl you in endless circles of questioning your very being, then you don't understand the reason for truth.

The truth is, God knows who we are even when we do not. He accepts us as we are because He see us as He created us to be, not as we have crafted ourselves. Isn't it odd we think God should change Himself and approve of us rather than that we should change to be approved?

And that's the truth, which, by the way, sets us free.

Then you will know the truth, and the truth will set you free.
-- John 8:32

One more thing about real truth: it will not taunt you or tantalize you because it has no need to make itself attractive. It just is, after all, *the* truth. It doesn't have to dress up and make promises beyond the one that Jesus Himself made: it sets us free.

I would rather run wildly through the wilderness with my hands in the air and my voice crying out for rescue in pursuit of truth as the hounds of hell bark at my heels than sit in the camouflaged comfort of surrendering to world-inflicted wounds now soothed by the balm of something I know is not from God. How far you enter into the "age of enlightenment" depends on how ignorant you can convince yourself to be about the Word of God.

If God had not already cornered the market on truth, we might have some merit for embracing it from elsewhere or even creating it ourselves. Instead, we need to accept it.

I don't know why some of us find ourselves so at odds with God's clear direction. Yes, I believe He could have sorted a few sins out of the mix. I would have voted for the elimination of sexual brokenness of all kinds so we could all live happily ever after in perfect harmony, with no one conspicuously drifting off key. Let something else be the greatest sin . . . okay? Let someone else be the most naked.

No, I think we are so much better off battling to the very end if that is necessary than we will ever be just seeking an end, at all costs, to this battle. The truth is, only God knows when you will be free of it, but, if you turn your longings elsewhere, forsaking the paths of righteousness for the personal path of what seems right to you or others, you may find yourself in unwelcome wilderness. When you find yourself with a choice between the wilderness and the door, dig deep for the key.

Stand at the crossroads and look; ask for the ancient paths, ask where the good way is, and walk in it, and you will find rest for your souls.
-- Jeremiah 6:16

Stand.
Look.
Ask.
Walk.
Rest.

Now that's the naked truth.

CHAPTER 24

THE BLESSED AFFLICTION OF A CONFLICTED HEART

What if the lines in the sand just keep shifting?
What if the boundaries we set up keep slipping?
What if the truth we've been seeking keeps drifting?
What if we don't make it through all this sifting?

What if our reach leaves us grasping at air?
What if our longing finds no one there to share?
What if our damage seems too much to repair?
What if we outrun those still willing to care?

But, what if we make our way into the clearing?
And what if we reject all the lies we've been hearing?
What if we surrender the things we've been fearing?
And, what if we let Someone else do the steering?

What if we truly believe what He told us?
What if we allow Him to mend us and mold us?
And what if we let His great grace so enfold us
That we could be free from the "what ifs" that hold us?

What if?

For I do not do the good I want to do, but the evil I do not want to do
-- this I keep on doing. -- Romans 7:19

Why does evil so often win the want-to war?

When I look back on the many opportunities I've had to "do the good I want to do," and done it not, but instead, with a less-and-less-trembling hand chose the more harmful but seemingly more momentarily-satisfying evil, I am startled at the efficiency with which that evil, almost unimpeded, made its way through my life, hacking away the tender shoots of hope which dared to break the dry and packed-down soil on which I trod in search of fleeting satisfaction.

That's *if* I look back. Evil would have me not do even that, but instead let bygones be bygones, memories rest in disrepair, miserable failings masquerade as best intentions. Oh, well. What could I have done differently, anyway? We are who we are. Right?

Wrong. Like evil.

I faced temptations common to man and gave in to them. I faced choices and, with measured but dismissed reluctance, made bad ones. I saw the risks and took the leaps and left loved ones behind on the outer bank. I knew good and wanted it . . . but did bad and hated it . . . and still wanted it.

I do indeed believe in forgiveness and repentance, healing and cleansing . . . a new beginning. But what to do about what was done before . . . or . . . even worse . . . since? The truth is, even in the best of us, evil lies in wait and trips us up and leaves us pining away or clamoring after the lesser things. We are not beyond being base again. Sometimes we still decide we want to be who we were instead of who we have become.

Thank God for conflict. It pulls us back; it pulls us forward. It should put us in permanent pursuit of peace.

And then, there's the "enlightened" culture. Addicted to conflict, culture slyly applies it, selectively, succumbing to the seductiveness of evil. And culture just keeps on keeping on, while the church, ever-trying to be relevant, resists taking a stand,

129

protecting the payments on the pews over the people sitting in them. Heaven forbid. Please.

Even the conflicts between church and culture that do go on are elevated to a higher plane, almost like a no-fly zone, while the combat goes on down here on the ground, in the conflicted hearts of Christians closer to the exit than the pulpit. We counter-attack culture with committee reports and resolutions, as it marches on and over us, gaining more and more territory, redefining truth and seeking to make everyone feel good, every sense titillated and satisfied. If culture wins, we'll all love ourselves and love our neighbors, but not exactly in the way God intended when He said we should.

As the church sits, dependent on divine intervention, culture chomps on at the pillars of life. Reluctant to be the tools of the Divine, we look on in dismay. Somebody, we say, should do something. We need to be ready to put feet beneath our prayers.

Distancing ourselves from the dirty deeds around us is not enough. We may find ourselves with clean hands, but those among us who are melding with the mud need someone daring to pull them out and steady their feet as they slowly walk away from the slippery bank.

Why are we more willing to raise funds and lift prayers for trips to foreign lands than we are to lift those around us out of the darkness? If you're sitting in the light because of God's grace, use it to help vanquish the shadows that surround you.

Again . . . thank God for the conflicted heart. If it did not exist within us, imagine how many more Christians would yield to the siren call of culture, the promise of acceptance, a place to openly go, no more hiding. At various times in life, it appealed even to me. My conflicted heart would look upon those in the gay community who seem to be so secure in who they are. Always going out, laughing, meeting for breakfast, taking in a movie, off on a trip somewhere . . . ever-smiling, smug in a greater enlightenment and understanding of what it means "to be."

Whatever unhappiness invades their lives is not their fault, they say, but just a result of the oppressiveness of culture and the ignorance of Christians who adhere to a skewed version of scriptural truth. Culture and pro-gay advocacy are so intertwined now that they are truly inseparable. They espouse a life of "surely

God meant," instead of "surely God said." Lives based solely on want can never be satisfied, for there is nothing greater than what I need, what I think and my freedom to do whatever I choose.

They not only want no conflict; they don't want you to have any either. Like a mermaid sitting on a rock, they call you into drowning with promises of the best swim of your life.

Only when we, as Christians, begin recognizing the afflictions of our brothers and sisters, sons and daughters, husbands and wives, mothers and fathers, fellow reflections of the image of Christ, will we make any inroads against the unrelenting march of culture.

Are we brave enough?
Do we care enough?
Can we love enough?
Forgive enough?
Believe enough?

As we stand warily by, culture's vultures descend on the wounded among us and mock our truths with shades of such, offering their own brands of courage, caring, love, acceptance and believe-in-yourself messages that sound all-too-appealing to the downtrodden hiding behind the hope of praise songs, wishing someone would take their hand and keep them from sliding from the pew into the pit.

We can do this, you know?

I can do all things through Him who strengthens me. -- Philippians 4:3

That's not a verse for selective application. It says "all." Yes, it applies to the struggler who needs to resist temptation. You can't imagine how many times it has been repeated in prayer in the dead of night in the midst of great conflict. But it is also a verse that needs to be applied to the silent Christian who has by the grace of God escaped sexual brokenness, but who folds his hands in the very shadow of the struggler and fails to take a stand -- not just on the truth -- but on the love of Christ. Instead, too many just stand by, unwilling to walk with the broken one, side-

131

by-side, aware of the cost of conflict, but ever-sure of the outcome when we trust and obey.

We could set an example there: "trust and obey."

The line in the sand is shifting. Where do you stand?

CHAPTER 25

WHAT IF IT WAS ONLY "ALMOST?"

As far as I know -- for not all dreams are remembered -- I've never dreamed of Easter. I've acted in church plays from high school, where I played a very youthful Jesus, to middle-age, playing Paul, in a costume with a close resemblance to Fred Flintstone. If that had been a dream, I would have gladly awakened.

I've tried to project myself into the scene while watching other actors re-enact Christ's death in churches and on the big screen, but I always feel short of really capturing in my mind what it must have been like, from the triumphant entry to the triumphant victory. It's impossible to capture the perspective, realizing when we re-enact it, we do so with the fullness of a truth the real witnesses did not have. We know how the story reconciles itself. For us, it is not an "Oh, my God" moment with exclamation points and question marks, shouts and tears. It's a God moment. A simple period of awe suffices.

I feel almost like I cheated somehow, not having to endure the roller-coaster ride of emotions that had to have completely drained those involved, from the owner of the donkey to the owner of the tomb, from the Garden of Gethsemane to the pensive upper room. I get the heart-saving benefits of their experience without the heart-stopping moments.

Of course, we have the Word. We can read of the painful and horrifying crucifixion, Peter's woeful sobbing through denials while a cock crows in acknowledgement of how far he has fallen, of those who fled into hiding, lost in confusion while the seemingly-defeated Messiah begins to decay in a dark and guarded tomb. We can read also of the brilliant sunrise reflecting on a rolled-away stone and an empty grave and imagine the shouts of glory from those who were first to know with absolute certainty that Jesus was and is and always will be.

I didn't get to be among the first to run screaming "He's Alive!" Emerging from the darkness of mourners' distress into the light of the reality of holiness, those who knew Him first could contain their joy no more than the grave could contain the Lord. I can put myself in their places and imagine the wash of relief and the dispensation of doubt forever. "Look . . . it is Him."

Maybe I have never dreamed of it because it is so real and so right and so righteously radiant in truth that no unlimited deep-sleep fascination can do it justice. Even the best of "dreams" are only what might be, what almost could happen.

In a dream, if I were to find myself among the mob, I could *almost* count the strikes of the whip; *almost* see the spit flying, *almost* share the hidden fear and pain of those who watched their hopes and dreams stumble in the dust beneath the weight. I could *almost* see Christ's eyes fill with salty sweat I could not wipe away for Him. I could *almost* see him look at me through waves of pain, gazing down in mercy. I could *almost* imagine the labored breathing and I could *almost* shed the tears of those who stood in the shadows beyond the spears. I could *almost* hear Him cry out, reflecting His sorrow at the silence of God who had to turn away from his cry for His will to be done. I could *almost* grasp the heavy finality of the massive stone inflicting blackness on the darkened tomb holding a withered man and all the weary misery of the world. I could *almost* feel the evil as it pushed against the stone to hold Him in, minions prepped for a victory pose, ready to move out and lay waste to the misguided mourners and reinforce the spoils of death. And then, I could *almost* bear the brilliance of Christ's victory, my salvation, and the force of a new round of nails now posting for all to see the death sentence for evil.

He is not here; He has risen! Remember how He told you, while He was still with you in Galilee: 'The Son of Man must be delivered into the hands of sinful men, be crucified and on the third day be raised again.' "
– Luke 24:6-7

But my eyes are open, not closed. I am awake and well beyond the third day. Because of Christ, *almost* has becomes *always.*

We can *always* know that we are worth everything He went through. In His "alwaysness," we can *always* call on Him to help us to live as He did . . . according to the perfect will of His . . . our . . . Father in heaven.

Always.

We can *always* live knowing He loves us and He gave Himself for us. And when we fail to love others as He did and does, we can always depend on His forgiveness and His help to forgive others as He did and does. To encourage others as He did and does.

Always.

And in times of trouble, which He knows will *always* be with us; we will *always* know He is as well.

Jesus never almost did anything.

It's an ever thing for everyone. The love that led Him through the streets; sustained Him in the beatings; filled his lungs with labored breath; rode the waves of wracking pain; drowned out the sound of the hammer; bore up beneath the searing sun; defied the evil victory chants of Satan; burst forth in direct proclamation . . . was for you and me.

When it seems we can only *"almost"* do those things He *always* does -- show mercy, extend grace, seek righteousness, forgive again, sin no more -- He is always there to wipe the tears, carry the burden, open the door, mend the relationship, dispel the fear, denounce the doubt, heal and restore the hope. More strength, more guidance; more clarity; *always* His supply is endless. His truth *always* enduring.

To those who drift in the *almost* of Easter, it is a dreamy celebration of floppy ears and colored eggs, chocolate candy and perfect pictures posed in Sunday best. An imagining of how life should be, all sugar-coated smiles and starched clean dreams. It may work for the day, but it is a broken token in comparison to the eternity of *always*.

Truth trumps dreams and all imaginings.

We do not have to *dream or imagine* God left His throne for us; we can know He did.

We do not have to *dream or imagine* Christ looks at us with the same mercy He did the one who pierced His side; We know He does.

We do not have to *dream or imagine* Christ forgives us as clearly and completely as He did the repentant man on the cross at his side; we know He does.

I do not have to *dream or imagine* the very aim of His death was our salvation; we know it was.

I do not have to *dream or imagine* we will one day stand before Him to join in perfect praise in person to Him our gratefulness for His stepping free of His tomb. We know we will.

We cannot *dream or imagine* Christ died, defeated death and rose. And we cannot just imagine why. It was because He loves us and only He could save us. We can't save ourselves. He knew that; He did that.

Jesus knew that every step He took and every word He spoke would eventually take Him to the cross, to the tomb, through death and back to the throne. As He walked the route, He knew us at every stop along the way, just as He knows us at every stumble, victory, climb, and tumble along our circuitous route to meet Him at His throne. He knows us now. He loved us always; always will.

Jesus never *almost* did anything.

CHAPTER 26

DON'T BELIEVE
THE BELIEF THIEVES

My father died 24 years ago at the age of 60 on a day I did not notice, busy with my own life, far removed from his. It shouldn't have been that kind of day. There was no late night bedside call for a last-gasp farewell. I did not even know he was so close to death, and, I fear, had he lived another decade, I would have known no more in 1998 than I did in 1988. At some point, I became so focused on him not being a good father that I completely neglected being a good son.

I believed I had done what was best, surrendering to his belligerent determination to live life on his own terms, which turned out to be short-term. I'm not sure what *he* believed because I had long since quit asking or wondering or wanting to know.

That was wrong.

So many things we do or accept are wrong, based on something we have been told we should believe, or on something we have been told we should not. Or just some inner feeling. Or perhaps the babble of someone who will feel no loss from our bad-belief-based decisions. For instance, my children never met my father because I "believed" it was best. Now that I myself know what it feels like to have grandchildren withheld, I understand the impact of my self-righteous decision to "protect" them from exposure to a broken-down alcoholic who would never so much as buy them a dollar toy, but would have perhaps seen hope within them that he could not find on the cold dark streets of Fort Worth, Texas . . . or in me and my self-righteousness.

Oh what dangers lurk in what we think is best for others.

I'm not saying we necessarily have to walk a mile in a man's shoes to have any say about the direction in which he is traveling. If so, we'd all be so deep in sin, trying to gain relevant experience, we would be collectively immobile and life would end. My father was uneducated, fought in World War II, endured a divorce and lost his wife and kids to a more promising man who dealt promises out like a worn deck of cards and never followed through on a one that I know of. My father spent a bit of time in jail on occasion and considered himself meaner than hell, despite an overall gentle nature of which others took advantage. He began drinking in his early years and likely died with a finished bottle at his side. I don't want to walk in those shoes; it was better he be buried in them.

I believed he would never recover. I believed he did not care about me. I believed it was best to cut ties. I believed that if he really wanted a life, he would get after it, get over it, get on with it. That's all past tense. I believe now that he came to believe he could not recover because no one believed he could. I believe he decided to stop expressing care for me because he believed I wanted nothing to do with him. I believe he just . . . died, and that he probably wondered what took so long.

I believe that sometimes what we believe about others robs them of any hope of believing in themselves.

My father never knew I struggled with unwanted same-sex attraction, but I believe he would have understood, and, in his own addiction, would have seen my struggle and, I believe, he would have encouraged me to not give in or give up. He would not have been dismissive either, just saying "get over it." I don't think he would have labored with his own beliefs over the issue, but would have instead focused on me.

Of course, I can believe these things because he is not here. One of the most difficult things anyone with sexual brokenness – which includes many Christians, especially with pornography -- has to deal with, is the constantly trumpeted and trumping beliefs of those who *are* here, whittling away at the struggler's belief that

God can heal and change and is patient and loving. The God who saw the first flicker of skewed sexuality grow into a flaming and consuming inner fire which controls you . . . is the same God who will snuff out the last ember as freedom comes. I believe that and no one is taking that belief from me.

If you or someone you know struggles, believe that God can and will set you free in His time and in His way if you are faithful to follow Him, confess your failings, seek forgiveness, repent and keep walking. As you walk, keep an eye out for the people who can take this belief from you and leave you hopelessly clinging to a diminished God. Can we not just believe together that without God, we're toast? Sin does not mend at our own demand.

The motives differ, but truth suffers when you deal with any of the many "belief thieves."

Recruiters. These people will do anything to tempt you into acting out on your sexual temptations, especially if you are porn-addicted. To them, you are only as valuable as the next click. Under the mask of "meeting your natural need," they are trading you around like a fading baseball card. You mean less to them than even the people they manipulate into "entertaining" you. Whatever your sexual problem is, someone out there knows how to make you feel better, as long as you make *them* feel better. These recruiters are users producing losers.

Refuters. These are the people who refuse to believe you have any problem at all. "Don't worry; be happy." "Smile and the world smiles with you." "Accept yourself." They revise the truth of the Bible in pursuit of that all-important happiness and really don't want to be pulled down by you plodding along your path to wholeness. You know how it is . . . people who are dissatisfied with themselves can be *so* dreary. You pour out your soul and they respond with a queasy "don't do that." The tempting thing about refuters and their redefining of God's Word is that it can be tempting to believe what masquerades as relieving reassurance.

Recusers. These are the people who approach you with a "get thee behind me" look. They wash their hands of you and shake the dust off their feet fairly quickly and then pledge to pray, but also say "people like you don't ever change." This proclamation says more about *their* faith than yours, as they have somehow divinely reckoned that God is not . . . divine. He can create a universe, but he cannot change you? That's definitely a get-thee-behind-me thought.

Reminders. These are the people who like to remind you that not only have you been bad, you redefined bad and your picture made its way into the dictionary. They remember every slip, every dip, every lie and every try that did not work, and, lest you get giddy about shaking off a bit of the slime of the past, they've got barrels of it stored in the garage. They use that to dash your hopes, lest you forget how much you hurt them. You can confess; you can repent; they'll never relent.

The one thing all of these people have in common is the belief that they have it right. Forgive them for that, but realize that their beliefs are not rooted so much in love the need for self-assurance about their rightness. What we need are people who are Christ-like, sacrificial, not seeking anything in return. That's a lot to ask for from people, but there are some who love you enough to take up that task. Look for them.

Be one of them.

We move beyond the shame and the guilt of being sexually-broken when we move into the reality that Christ -- who hates sin and clearly knows the cost because He paid the price -- is not surprised by our brokenness, devastated by our stubbornness, disturbed by our sinfulness, or deaf to our cries for restoration. The One who is all and knows all, loves all and died for all, does not recuse Himself from our case, refuse our pleas, remind us of our confessed sins or seek to justify them for the sake of happiness and inner peace. You and I are the all.

Yes, we do need people. The days of our lives should not play out unnoticed. But it is okay, even for the broken, to be discerning, building relationships with people who will look you in the eye and nod in agreement with you when you tell them that you believe you can be free. Later, when you believe that you are, you can work on those recruiters, refuters, recusers and reminders. They need your help.

Keep the faith.

CHAPTER 27

SELF AND TEMPTATION: 'TILL DEATH DO WE PART

I used to have this thing for hot spicy Doritos and sweet Hostess Twinkies. The crisp flavor-packed chips and the cream-filled soft fluffy cakes would call out my name every time I would pass a 7-11. In the bigger grocery store, they were only an aisle or two away from fresh fruits and vegetables, and so convenient, often even on sale. They beckoned from the pantry at home. The popping of the tab on a Diet Dr. Pepper was the starting gun for a race to down a bag of chips and couple of Twinkies. I would justify the chips by using them to scoop up tuna. How bad could that be? The Twinkies? Well, you have to do something to satisfy a severely-challenged sweet tooth that has endured peppered tuna and a bit of picante.

Somewhere along the line I moved from sense-satisfying Doritos to sensible pretzels and then just pretty much dropped chips all-together. No more Twinkies either. Though I have been known to pause and even pick up a pack and read the nutrition label, I usually opt for an energy bar now. More expensive, less enjoyable, but much more sensible. Victory in the small things perhaps. Giving up the cakes and chips required absolutely no real deprivation whatsoever, and only a moderate amount of self-control, which, when exercised, actually works.

So, first God fills the world with incredibly wonderful things, then Satan comes along and sows seeds of corruption among all the good things so we have to rummage among the thorns. Getting what we want is suddenly painful and requires major maneuvering skills. Then God tells us that we will be tempted and Satan takes full advantage of *that* truth and we maneuver our way somehow through the good and the bad and partake 'till our bodies, our minds, or our spirits are bloated to the point of implosion. Self and temptation: 'till death do we part. In a constant and consistent effort to please ourselves, we eat and drink and stimulate every pleasurable sense we possess far beyond the good sense we often don't.

If it were not so, I would not tell you.

In the common marriage of misfits, person and poison just seem to go together. From the baby in the high chair who just can't stop flinging the peas onto the floor to the sexually-addicted man or woman who cannot stem the flow of addictive pornography in the darkened room behind the locked door at the end of the hall. From the child who delights in spinning tall tales for attention to the local gossip who lies and destroys the lives of the ones she wishes would just love her. From the teenager who masturbates in solitude with a magazine fueling his fantasy to the man who cruises the local bars for today's take-home friend, a user-takes-all reality. From searching for fun to searching for satisfaction to searching for survival, we slowly succumb to the deeds of desire. When we finally ask ourselves how we got there, we can barely remember the first turn on to the road and the early warning signs have disappeared beneath the depths of despair to which they led.

Yes, it's dark. But . . . deprivation is so icky. Have a Twinkie. Or a trick.

Temptation is so pervasive that even those who seem above it are tempted to demonstrate their resistance and can soon find themselves falling prey to boasting and arrogance, unaware that they have become peacocks, unable to resist spreading their feathers for a look-at-me strut. Lord, please tempt a few more of them with an insatiable desire for humility.

Is there no hope on this dark twisting road -- this trail of temptation -- that trumps itself at each turn with wonders anew designed to undo?

No temptation has overtaken you except what is common to mankind. And God is faithful; He will not let you be tempted beyond what you can bear. But when you are tempted, He will also provide a way out so that you can endure it. -- 1 Corinthians 10:13

Now that is worth a pause along the path as we tiptoe through the tulips of temptation. Of course, by this time we may have grown a little averse to verses like I Corinthians 10:13 that start with "no," but do read on.

Your temptations are just common. -- That's right. Everything that beckons you is a been-there-done-that-over-and-over-again ploy. If there is nothing new under the sun, then the temptations that trail behind you to snare you as you weaken or the temptations that tarry on before you to trip you as you strengthen are just common old things that have emerged in the paths of every man and woman, Adam-and-Eve-on. *You're* special . . . but your temptations aren't.

God is faithful. -- Sometimes when I look at all the things we forfeit to satisfy the taunting of temptation, I want to hide from God in tears, unable to admit to Him that He gave me so much and I traded it away for . . . nothing. He loves us and we choose others to love above Him. He joins us with another and we choose to splinter the union until it sometimes gives way beneath the weight of all our wayward wants. We leave the garden in our own free will on way too many occasions and yet . . . God is faithful and plants new gardens of Grace in which we can be restored. He knows the validity of our confessions and accepts them even when others -- jaded by our failures -- turn away. He sees the reality of repentance even when others may refuse, reluctant to walk that road with us again. He cherishes the bruised reed and fans the smothered wick back to life.

God knows your limits. -- Face it, we don't. The Twinkie-hoarder doesn't see a 300-pound image in his future. The teen who grabs a Playboy from beneath his daddy's bed doesn't see himself someday isolated behind a screen, staring at naked men and women on a website, muttering "I'm busy" when his own children tap on his shuttered door. The "curious" and lonely young man or woman looking for acceptance through sexual exploration doesn't see a future of sexual addiction where the search for sensual satisfaction trumps any semblance of self-worth. It's all give and take, like some perverted poker game. But God always knew what you could endure and He always knew you could have turned the other way in time . . . and that you still can, in His time, not yours. The temptations -- those common things -- that have beset you and controlled you? God says you can rise above them.

God provides a way. -- To that, you might say, 'Oh yeah? Well, I've cried out for the way and as the cries fade, exhaustion ensues, temptation endures and I fall again." Let's face it, though. We haven't ended up in the perpetual u-turn of temptation by looking in all the right places. For crying out loud . . . it takes more than just crying out. God provides the way . . . but He doesn't smother you with it. God provides the way . . . but He doesn't wall you away from the world He created. God provides the way . . . but it's not a walk for the faint-at heart. The courage of confession is the entry ramp to the road of repentance . . . and it's a long-haul process. Don't blame God for the bumps you put in your path; ask him for the endurance you need to get beyond them.

You will still be tempted. -- He says in His Word, *"when* you *are* tempted." He didn't say if or maybe. I can think of a dozen things this very moment that tempt me . . . but I'm not going to share that with you because it could cause you to be tempted too. I don't know what your temptations are or what pulls your trigger, but God does, and He knows how to put it on safety because He knows you better than you do yourself because He doesn't resist knowing you . . . and sometimes you do. You *will* be tempted, by something, somewhere. Don't let it overtake you. Endure in God.

Here, in the heat of summer, with temperatures daily exceeding 100, it's really odd to pass the signs that precede each of the bridges on my way to and from the office: "Bridge Ices Before

Road." In this current season, those signs don't cause me to slow down or proceed with caution. I just whiz by, cross the bridge and head on down the road. Life is filled with seasons, though, and sometimes those bridge signs are deep with meaning.

Just heading on down the road? I'm afraid that's what we often do with the warning signs that precede the bridge that takes us down the ever-darkening road of temptation. If we would remember that the bridge ices before the road, maybe we would slow down, or turn back, take a different route and seek the truth of Christ's love, which would thaw out the bitterness in our hearts that tells us we have every right to fulfill ourselves by feasting on our temptations rather than on His guidance. After all, we've all been down that road before, and we know well the eventual slide into the ditch that comes when the force of want exceeds the grip of self-control. Instead of heeding the warning signs, we end up calling for a tow.

Your temptations may follow you all of your life, but God is greater, more ever-present, acts only in your best interest, gives His Spirit to guide you, unfolds the map, provides all the bridges, lays out all the paths and is leaving the light on to rejoice when you arrive at the place beyond all temptations. We *can* endure this road.

In the meantime, if anyone ever tells you that they've have mastered all temptation, suggest they read the Bible and then be willing to man the tow truck when the time comes and they find themselves stuck on a lonely shoulder of some one-way highway. This is a long journey, but there are no bridge-free roads.

CHAPTER 28

SOMETIMES I FEEL LIKE A HOUSE

For we know that if the earthly tent we live in is destroyed, we have a building from God, an eternal house in heaven, not built by human hands. – 2 Corinthians. 5:1

I have at times in the past skated on very thin ice, life-speaking. I have also been tested by fire and occasionally found lacking. I have been cold and I have been warm and I have been luke . . . as in lukewarm, somewhere in the sad and unsatisfying middle. But not long ago, as Christmas closed in, I was at peace, almost overwhelmed by the incredible undeniable truth that wherever and whenever, I am never alone. And never will be.

On a peaceful Saturday night, one week before Christmas, around 10:30 p.m., our house went up in flames. Five hours later, with smoke still rising from the ashes of a few glowing spots set against the dark horizon, we viewed from our rear-view mirror -- as we drove down our street -- the grey piles of decades of memories being sifted by the night's cold wind . . . and we took them with us. Memories.

The charred rafters poked into the night toward the stars like ribs from a skeleton, having surrendered the contents of an attic filled with the scrapbooks and collected "stuff," of college, courtship, marriage, the raising of five children, all the good things sifted and saved from the ups-and-downs of life lived together . . . in a house that is no more. Star Wars toys and baby dolls, baseball cards and baby books, all the "mines" that became one big "ours." The first-owners of the precious things grew up and moved on to other precious things, leaving behind little monuments to the pieces of days that form a history of a family, not completely-told. We have a tendency to bar from the attic the times of heartache and let them dwell more personally in our minds. Attics, while always portrayed as foreboding and frightening, are usually filled with the better things of life, the fragments we hold on to for the peace they bring us when we picture them there or dig through to hold them briefly once again.

In the unrelenting and indiscriminating fire, colorful plastics and bright fabrics become grey; photos curl and blacken and turn to dust. Oft-used and carefully-preserved baby furniture turns crisp and crumbles into a wind-sifted mix with everyday un-notables like ironing boards and end-tables. And finally, the "things" of life are matted into the melted carpet by gallons and gallons of water until the precious mixes with the priceless and the pointless to make a porridge, a gooey, sticky paste upon the floor.

All gone.

Stuff.

Forever in the rear-view mirror, no matter how many circles we make to try to come in around before the fire.

Adios, stuff.

Now, don't get me wrong. I miss the stuff, but I miss greater things. We lost a lot, but we have endured greater loss before. I would like some of the stuff back into my life, but not as much as I want something else -- someone else -- back. Make that plural. People away long before the fire.

I guess I fear that a new attic on a new house may remain too empty.

Three days passed and the house did not rise, proving once again that if we worship stuff, we ourselves may someday just be more of the mix of grey. Though the house did not rise, the sun did, right there where it always does, just to the east of the piece of land on which the house stood.

What good is a fire -- or any seemingly-destructive moment in our lives -- if we don't try to see in it how God is able?

Able to take those ashes that look like "the end" to us and work His endless beginnings again? What good is searing heat without eye-opening light? What good is a look into the rear-view mirror if it is not to safely change lanes and proceed? What good is it to lose all that old stuff if we forget that He is always making all things new?

At night, when there is nothing more to do, I think through the why and come up with . . . whatever? Mental flexing won't re-mix mortar or re-frame walls that aren't there anymore no more than it will take down walls still there that you wish were not. But still, you can't help but wonder and though God is the God of all Wonders, the devil of doubt likes to use them too.

Such as . . .

Maybe this was somehow my fault? Not, fault as in, did I leave a burner on (I didn't), or put something too close to a heater (nope) or . . . whatever . . . nada. In fact, I was simply watching a less-than-a-barn-burner basketball game on TV and smelled something burning. That simple. The "fault" questions plague the mind at midnight because, no matter how fully aware we are of forgiveness, we sometimes think we *deserve* every bad thing that happens to us, as if God sits with a scorecard and realizes all of a sudden we need a holy zap. I'm not talking about the natural consequences that arise from our sins, but just the general late-night idea that, because we failed and turned away in the past, we are doomed to encounter all kinds of dreadful things in the future, as if, somehow past bad judgment and temptation-succumbing should just naturally lead to a house-fire. "*I deserve this.*" Nope. I deserved lots of things that were specifically connected to my sins, but the towering inferno is not one of those things. God doesn't work that way. Our lives may seemingly go up in smoke because of sexual sin, but our house is not predestined to flash into flames. Bad things and good things happen to good people and bad. They just do. There's no reason to fan the flames. The devil likes to fill our minds with doleful tales of doubts about what we've done and who we are and what we've brought upon ourselves to bring us down to the putrid depths of the distant dark in which he dwells. No doubt about it; the devil hates us.

149

God works to restore us, reserving mansions because He loves us.

Maybe God will work a miracle? Maybe. Maybe not. Miracle-musing at midnight fades in the brightness of the realistic dawn. God can do anything. He could use this tragedy to fulfill a wish list or answer a prayer. He *could.* These moments work in movies and books to round out the tragedy of the plot and bring everyone home in a group-hug moment of awakening, forgiveness and a furious re-building of relationships. The important thing in real life for the Christian -- no matter how terribly checkered or how nearly flawless the life lived so far -- is to trust and obey. Expectations built on that foundation are always met. "Trust and Obey" are not lyrics or simple inspiring words, they are God's Word, strong and mighty. He just naturally likes us to do what He knows is best for us.

Maybe I'm just cursed? If so, a quick read of the morning paper puts me in good company. If all the afflicted are cursed, the crowd is approaching a point beyond control. The pain some people bear these days before Christmas makes my "stuff," seem less than minimal and my focus on it purely dismal and dumb. In a world full of people who thirstily pant for peace, chaos too often reigns.

Maybe . . . maybe I should just drop all the maybes altogether and celebrate the blessings I have because they are too many to count.

No maybe about this: I have a wonderful wife -- Lisa -- who truly does see beauty rising from ashes and is patient enough to wait for others to clue in to the view.

No maybe about this: I have friends. I have neighbors. I have family. Good and loving people, whether they're in Norman, Oklahoma or Faridpur, Bangladesh, Cincinnati or Columbia, Seattle or London, Texas or Tennessee, Alaska or Australia. God's house is really big, and it stands. And encourages. And helps. And loves.

Which leads me back to the blessings. And peace. For some reason, I have a feeling this past Christmas will rank a bit higher in my memory even than the year I got the hamster . . . and, at that time of life, I could not see how that could ever be topped.

God was with *me*, not stored in the attic. He was not framed in by the flaming walls. He does not drift away on clouds of smoke into the night and His brightness does not fade no matter how blazing the rising or setting of the sun, just one of His many handiworks.

God has a way of taking away doubts and maybes and replacing them with truths.

Sometimes you have to be taken back down to the foundation so everything can become new. Refurnished, fresh, the old removed, the walls strong, the clutter turned to ashes.

Sometimes I just feel like a house.

CHAPTER 29

WAIT FOR THE WHISPER

Even youths grow tired and weary, and young men stumble and fall; but those who hope in the Lord will renew their strength. They will soar on wings like eagles; they will run and not grow weary, they will walk and not be faint. -- Isaiah 40:30-31

The man slept. Finally. His body had pleaded; his mind had relented; his spirit was depleted and his heart had retreated, so he slept. It was restless, not restful, and the dreams were not sweet, but instead added to the eventual misery of awakening, leaving him already tired upon rising. The few things he did not constantly replay while awake whirled through his unprotected mind in sleeping, magnified by the mysterious melding of reality and fantasy, leaving him wondering if there was any need at all to emerge again beneath the deep of sleep. But, then again, sleep was never really deep anymore.

In the light of the unwelcome day he heard his mind's relentless voice of repetitive remorse remind him of his losses, his misses, his self-inflicted misery, his many moments off-the-mark. Sitting still seemed the safest way to face a future that seemed to promise only more loneliness, more unanswered questions. Frozen, he believed that any action now might cause him to veer further off course and become more and more hopeless. So he did nothing. He just waited, anticipating his next fall, some greater stumble.

"I am so tired," he sighed to the man inside.

But Someone else heard, and whispered "I am your strength."

The boy woke. Finally. He peeked through the blinds of his bedroom window to see the morning sun filtering through the branches of the trees that lined his street. His hair was soon combed; his book bag stuffed; his shoes tied. He could hear the rattle of cereal bowls down the hall; a dog barking in the yard and cars passing through the street. Soon he would hear a bell ring and take his seat and sigh and wonder why it was so wrong for boys to cry. The pain of loneliness made him more aware of and even more unsure of his heart.

In the light of the unwelcome morning, his little mind's relentless voice of repetitive remorse reminded him of his losses, the things he missed, the things he would miss out on, the calculated actions of the abuser who had taken advantage of his vulnerability, leaving him adrift in confusion, the slowly-creeping cracks threatening to ravage all the boyishness, crumbling him into a hellishness he could not comprehend.

"Where can I hide?" he sighed to the boy inside.

But Someone else heard, and whispered "In me."

The young woman rose. Finally. She turned away from the mirror and gazed down the hall towards the front door through which she could see the sun beginning to set behind the house across the street. Her hair was brushed; her face made up, her clothes finally on. She looked around her room at the piles of rejected garments, the too-little-girly, the not-quite-right. She could hear her mother on the phone, laughing; her father in his office, typing. In her room at the end of the hall it was so quiet she could almost hear her tears fall against the tight black blouse she had chosen because she thought it showed her . . . at her best.

In the fading light of the early dusk, her restless mind's relentless voice of repetitive remorse reminded her of her losses, the things she wished and now knew were beyond the hope of wanting, replaced instead by an endless desire to be loved or at least desired. She reached the door, paused to say goodbye, thought better of it and headed out into the night, lingering in the soft light of the porch to dab her eyes.

"Who wants me?" she sighed to the little girl inside.

But Someone else heard, and whispered "I do."

I wonder what life would be like if we never grew tired, never stopped so weary we can scarcely catch our breath? What if we walked without stumbling and never kissed the hard road of life with a face-first fall? No prodigals or wandering sheep; no one who needed to be called down from a tree or helped into a boat from storm-tossed waves. No need to lift our eyes to meet another's. No trembling last-ditch reach for the hem of a passing garment. No pleas; no cries. Would we waltz through the world like graceful dancers on a polished floor, knowing there would be no concerns about stepping out of tune? Or we would crash like puppets cut loose from strings, lifeless to the floor?

We couldn't hope in anything beyond our well-honed abilities; our own limited but safe strength. We could not fly; we dare not run. We'd never push our limits. We'd see our reach and never stretch beyond it. Safe and secure within our self-styled boundaries, we might cherish our non-skinned knees and walk on, but we would never soar. Whether in the brightness of the morning, the light of mid-day or the descending darkness of dusk, we would tell ourselves "this is my life," and we would listen for others to join in and build a chorus of acceptance, an embrace of lessness.

Tired.

Lonely.

Unwanted.

Looking for a hiding place instead of grace; searching for hole to climb into instead of hope to rise up in.

Just a whisper shy of soaring.

The man picked up the phone. Finally. As the soft rain pattered against the panes of his office windows, he searched through the contacts, paused, started to push the buttons and held his breath, half-hoping that if he did, there would be no answer at the other end as he called his old friend to offer his hand or his shoulder . . . or his love and support . . . whatever was needed to help him walk out of the endless circle of his sexual addiction. But . . . the visions of what his friend had done, who he'd hurt, what he had rejected, what he had chosen, what he had said . . . flooded his mind.

"I don't know how to do this," he sighed to the man inside.

But Someone else heard, and whispered "I do."

The father parked the car. Finally. Leaning forward, he rested his head against the steering wheel and placed his hands on the dash and rehearsed his speech, trying to hear it as an eight-year-old might, wondering what words he could use to re-build the trust, show his love, sow new seeds of security, carry for his beloved son the pain that threatened to suffocate the little boy's soul. His efforts to be real and good and strong and present began to weaken beneath his own guilt for his own great unraveling that had undone the safety of the life in which his son had once paraded.

"I don't know what to say to my own son," he sighed to the dad inside.

But Someone else heard, and whispered, "I do."

The mother heard the door softly shut and she told her friend on the phone to hold on as she peeked through the curtains and saw her daughter poised on the top step looking briefly back at the door she had closed behind her. She saw the pretty eyes from which a soft tear dropped and heard her friend on the phone saying "hey, are you there?" Her feet seemed a part of the carpet, unmovable, her hands frozen, her mind blocked, her heart restrained by memories of past moments of confrontation.

"I don't know how to love her anymore," she said to the mom inside.

But Someone else heard, and whispered "I do."

And surely I am with you always, to the very end of the age.
-- Matthew 28:20

Always?
When we are tired?
When we want to hide?
When we feel unwanted?
When we don't know what to do?
When we don't know what to say?
When We don't know how to love?
When . . . ever.

"Those who hope in the Lord will renew their strength."

When we find ourselves overwhelmed by what we have done, or by what has been done to us, or by what we have done to others or by what we failed to do, we need to admit our weariness, our tiredness, our emptiness, our falseness, our callousness, our sadness, our hatefulness, our lovelessness, our aimlessness . . . or whatever ness inflicts us and seek His wholeness and holiness.

Clear out the clutter, tune out the culture, pack away the pride . . . wait for Him to whisper.

He will.

CHAPTER 30

STRONGER THAN HELL

I can't remember ever doubting the existence of hell. As much as I believe "there is a God," I believe "there is a hell." I have no issue with the idea that "there is a judgment," either and that God decides who goes to hell, no matter how many times we may hear people throughout our lives telling others to "go to" or "burn in," or see someone wiping the sweat from their brows or the tears from their eyes, struggling to pick themselves back up after, saying "this is."

No, it's not.

I don't really like the idea of hell, but I accept it as part of God's plan . . . something not so much to be afraid of as to be freed from. It's not like He disguises it with camouflage bushes so we just skip along happily and suddenly tumble in. No, there are warning signs and a clearly marked exit ramp.

My real father joked about hell. He said he was too mean for hell. I think he believed in and feared it. I wish I could say for certainty he is not there. I hope that at some point in his up-and-down life he stepped off the roller coaster and met Jesus face to face. Again . . . I wish I knew for sure. I remember that when my dad left my life, when I was just a little boy, I might have thought -- but never said -- "this is hell." It wasn't, and, frankly, as sad as those days were, there would be more much worse. I think, in truth, hell is just hell. It doesn't get better; it doesn't get worse. It's just . . . hell.

My stepfather used to talk of hell too. To him, it was only an obscenity, to be uttered following "Oh," when he couldn't get a jar open or someone left a door ajar. If he was mad at something or someone, he would say "d*** it to hell," like he had some decision-making authority. I think he probably knows by now that he did not. He did make me pretty uptight about the word "hell" though. I put it on the list of things I could not say, along with other choice words from his vocabulary. It took me a long time to say "hell," and I only do it when talking about the real . . . hell, like I did in a chapter in *Surviving Sexual Brokenness*, called "If You're Going through Hell, Don't Stop at the Gift shop."

I remember, about the time I became a teenager, older guys, primarily college-age, were marching and chanting "Hell no, we won't go!" when President Lyndon Johnson escalated the war in Vietnam. But what I really remember is that my older brother didn't chant; he went. I think it was pretty close to hell for Mike, but it was the right thing for him to have gone . . . so it definitely was not hell, even if it felt like it.

My oldest son, Zach, participated in a bike race called Hotter'N Hell 100 in Wichita Falls. He endured rattlesnakes, dusty dry earth, perilous rocks and scorching sun and a really nasty injury in a wreck. It was hot, and I definitely don't want to go there, but it wasn't really hell. Or hotter than.

Though I pledged to not use the word, there have been plenty of times in my life when I should have looked around at where my sins had led me and said "Where in the hell am I?" It seems an appropriate question, for is there any place more lost than hell?

Well . . . that's probably enough about hell, except to explain why I chose to write about it anyway. Why? Because I know some people who are putting themselves through a personal hell, fenced in by shame and guilt, the breath of living sucked out of them by the weight of self-judgment, magnified by the imposed judgment of others.

Their spirits starve in hopelessness and they live in fear of the next fall as they see temptations swarming around them like, well . . . bats out of hell.

Who are they?

Porn addicts drifting further away from reality in darkened rooms behind computer screens, immersed in ever-elusive self-satisfaction. *("I'm not hurting anyone.")*

Christians battling unwanted same-sex attraction while sifting through culture-driven justification as a potential way out of the raging inner storm. *("You were born this way." "God wants you to be happy." "Christians are backward and narrow-minded.")*

Men and women giving in to lustful thoughts and slowly drifting in adulterous affairs. *("No one else understands me." "I'm going to stop this as soon as I can do it without hurting her . . . or him.")*

Maybe what they are going through is not technically hell, but it falls far short of heaven on earth. Maybe it is not real hell, but it feels like pure hell.

The sins are so easy to identify: fantasizing with porn, engaging in homosexuality, committing adultery. Fantasize. Engage. Commit. Not bad words on their own, but suffocating when paired with sexual sin. Nearly as suffocating as the words that often precede the giving in: lonely, rejected, abused, confused, longing, wanting, self-destructive.

These weak and wounded sinners are left by many to die. "We did our best to help. Now God will sort it out." Impatient at the sexually-broken's self-satisfying, fun-for-a-season descent into darkness, the also weak-and-wounded-in-other-ways watcher says . . . what? "Go to hell?" Or, maybe not. What if, aware of our own weaknesses, we pause, breathe, and say, with meaning that goes beyond all triteness: "God loves you and so do I," and extend the hand of grace and the embrace of love that is not like the love that the addicted seeks -- not a fantasy love -- but the love that heals, that is patient and kind and enduring. Christ-like love. No condoning, just compassion.

Can we love people when they have done wrong?

Can we not?

It takes energy to love someone who is draining all the life out of you through the exasperation of what seems like an embrace of sin. An embrace that is, in reality, more like an entanglement from which the sexual sinner exhausts himself fighting for freedom and then soothes the exhaustion with further strangling.

159

Jesus replied, "Blessed are you, Simon son of Jonah, for this was not revealed to you by flesh and blood, but by My Father in heaven. And I tell you that you are Peter, and on this rock I will build My church, and the gates of Hades will not overcome it." -- Matthew 16:17-18

I would like to have lived the kind of life where Jesus -- or anyone else, for that matter -- would refer to me as a rock . . . and not as a wayward pebble rolling down a slimy hill into the murky banks of a stagnant river going no-where. Sadly, plunking around me were pebbles sliding down from everywhere.

We are not stronger than hell, but Jesus is. He's been there and done that. And the church is. You and me, if we will just be . . . the church. Jesus said so.

Next time you see a lonely life-lost hitchhiker, perhaps in the pew beside you, or in the room down the hall, or the house down the street, with his thumb out and a life-sign that says "The Gates of Hell," pick him -- or her -- up. They may think they know where they're going because they or someone told them so. Help them toss their burdens in the trunk. Offer them truth to quench the thirst and give plenty of compassion to rest the soul. This truly is the long and winding road which seems to have no end when traveled alone. It's a no-passing zone and a lot of people are stuck in traffic.

The sexual sinner will suffer consequences . . . as will all who sin . . . you and I and everyone we know, but there is no sin beyond forgiveness. And I don't recall Jesus ever telling anyone "forget about it," when they truly sought His healing. The sexual sinner who knows the Lord is no more in danger of hell than the most near-perfect among us, so why not extend grace to each other and be busy at the work of plucking the pebbles from the brink?

What is hell on earth?

Really?

It is a place beyond grace.

Don't go there.

ENCOURAGING WORDS OF FAITH

CONSIDER HIDING THESE VERSES IN YOUR HEART

Then you will know the truth, and the truth will set you free.
-- John 8:32

Stand at the crossroads and look; ask for the ancient paths, ask where the good way is, and walk in it, and you will find rest for your souls. -- Jeremiah 6:16

I can do all things through Him who strengthens me.
-- Philippians 4:3

He is not here; He has risen! Remember how He told you, while He was still with you in Galilee: 'The Son of Man must be delivered into the hands of sinful men, be crucified and on the third day be raised again.' " – Luke 24:6-7

No temptation has overtaken you except what is common to mankind. And God is faithful; He will not let you be tempted beyond what you can bear. But when you are tempted, He will also provide a way out so that you can endure it.
-- 1 Corinthians 10:13

For we know that if the earthly tent we live in is destroyed, we have a building from God, an eternal house in heaven, not built by human hands. -- 2 Corinthians. 5:1

Even youths grow tired and weary, and young men stumble and fall; but those who hope in the Lord will renew their strength. They will soar on wings like eagles; they will run and not grow weary, they will walk and not be faint. -- Isaiah 40:30-31

And surely I am with you always, to the very end of the age. -- Matthew 28:20

Jesus replied, "Blessed are you, Simon son of Jonah, for this was not revealed to you by flesh and blood, but by My Father in heaven. And I tell you that you are Peter, and on this rock I will build My church, and the gates of Hades will not overcome it." -- Matthew 16:17-18

GRACE

CHAPTER 31

THE NEW MATH OF FORGIVENESS

Jesus said, "Father, forgive them, for they do not know what they are doing." -- Luke 23:34

Nothing hurts like hurting about hurts that make you hurt others. What a compound of pain that leads us to do unto others because something was done unto us and we've come all undone over it. So, we hurt and we cry and we ask ourselves why. And we hide and we run and we pray and we seek and we rise and we walk and we declare ourselves done. And then we see . . . we're not. For the carnage lies along the trail we yearn to leave behind and it calls out to us, to which we can only, in exhaustion from the battle, whisper in all sincerity, "please forgive me."

And we wait . . .

And the answer is . . .

Okay . . .

If . . .

And it is time to retrace our trail, trading the grace of redemption for the work of repairing, seeking to earn some measure of forgiveness as if it were a rare commodity to be extended only on completion of some arbitrary and man-ordained testing, a rite of passage for the one who truly shows he means it. Already finding ourselves barely breathing beneath the weight of the sorrow of sin's relentless pursuit and our weak attempts to escape, we dig our way out through the callused layers of repetitive sin, stand face-to-face with the reality of remorse and the challenge of repentance and ask . . . but do not receive. Spent, we engage in a new battle, so determined to prove ourselves worthy of that which seems to offer some hope of life: forgiveness.

Forgiveness does not fix sexual and relational brokenness. Forgiveness does, however, help remove the overwhelming obstacles of shame and guilt and lessen the likelihood of a u-turn. Powerful stuff forgiveness. Precious indeed. But it should be less rare and much more alive than the kajillion blades of grass in a dormant winter lawn. Imagine . . . 7 times 70 . . . times a billion or so people.

Forgiveness? God made plenty. It's a commodity that has flowed in un-stemmed abundance like a mighty timeless river straight from the gates of Eden, beneath the Cross of Christ and into the reservoirs behind the dams we've built to hold it back and make its power our own, to be administered when deserved according to our measured grace. "I'll forgive you when I know it won't come back to haunt me."

The new math of forgiveness. Seven times seventy has been replaced by a new equation. Once . . . maybe?

In a worst-case scenario, a sexually-broken person may have . . .

Engaged in clearly-sinful homosexual behavior, or . . .

traded the reality of life for the mindless pursuit of pornography, or . . .

committed adultery, bringing shame to his wife or her husband, or . . .

disintegrated into self-absorption through constant masturbation, or . . .

become mentally-entrenched in fantasizing over endless lustful pursuits . . .

accepting sexual addiction as self.

And these are just the non-criminal aspects of sexual brokenness. Homosexuality, pornography, adultery, self-satisfaction, lust, addiction. Which of these is unforgivable?

In your book?

In God's book?

When I was in high school, I had a dog named Sampson. I'd had a trying 15 years -- divorced parents, father abandonment,

166

sexual abuse, evil stepfather and ocean-deep instability -- and there was something indescribably comforting in the dog's soft brown eyes, lapping tongue, thick fur and bouncy eagerness. I was the most important thing to him. He couldn't wait for me to slip a leash onto his collar, unlock the gate, cross the street to the park and play. One day, while running with him in the park, he ran in front of me, distracted by some enticing sight. The leash wrapped around my legs and I fell . . . hard . . . on top of his soft brown body, snapping one of his legs beneath me.

He barked; he bit. I yelled; I nearly cried. I picked him up; he yelped. I said, "I'm sorry." He panted and licked my hand.

As Sampson healed, his surgically-reconstructed leg shaved and wrapped, he greeted me with the same wide tail wags that had always enticed me through the screen door and into the yard. There were no demands for proof I would never fall on him again. There was no penance. He didn't count the dog treats or analyze the sincerity of the petting.

Yes . . . I know. We're not dogs.

We're better. I can't help but believe that God expects a bit more from his greatest creation.

You see, Sampson was not attuned to the fine intricacies of forgiveness. He did not confuse it with repentance. He did not confuse it with consequences. He did not wonder if . . . if I was too-easily forgiven . . . I might take advantage of some future opportunity to snap his other legs. He didn't even know he was "forgiving" me. If there was any confusion on his part at all, it was between love and forgiveness, and that's not a bad mix-up to make.

Forgiveness is not a fool-me-once-shame-on-you, fool-me-twice-shame-on-me issue. We want to place it on the list of choices we have to make as persons rather than on the list of Christ-like attributes of surrendered person-hood. Christ never had to say "Do as I say, not as I do," when it came to forgiveness. He did and we must.

Forgiving someone does not mean they are free to cast aside the work of repentance. That work must still be done, but it is not dependent on you forgiving them. It may be, however, that the broken one sees a lack of forgiveness as an obstacle to the pursuit of repentance. Is that your problem? No . . . forgiveness is.

Forgiving someone does not mean they can cast aside the cost of the consequences. Burdens must be borne; penalties paid; costs calculated and debts repaid. Is that your problem? No . . . unless, in your forgiveness you discover a compassion that leads you to walk along the fallen from the crawling to the limping to the someday standing tall.

Forgiveness just means you forgive them, for Pete's sake. Or for their sake. Or for yours. Bearing the burden of unforgiveness can rival the impact of the original sin that brought down the reign of judgment. Even in the absence of repentance, even surrounded by the carnage of consequence, forgiveness reigns. It is the beginning of healing for both sides.

Better math.

Forgiveness doesn't always mean the complete restoration of your relationship with someone, but it helps clear a path, and is perhaps the only hope that your relationship will ever be rebuilt.

Maybe one of the more difficult circumstances under which we are called to forgive is when we look at someone who just seems to have been willingly and willfully sinning and hurting and pillaging life as if all of creation existed only for perverted pleasure. Forgive that? Take a cue from Christ. Forgiveness was dependent on some awareness or on a lack of.

Jesus said, "Father, forgive them, for they do not know what they are doing." -- Luke 23:34

And then, just a short time later:

One of the criminals who hung there hurled insults at Him: "Aren't you the Messiah? Save Yourself and us!" But the other criminal rebuked him. "Don't you fear God," he said, "since you are under the same sentence? We are punished justly, for we are getting what our deeds deserve. But this Man has done nothing wrong." Then he said, "Jesus, remember me when you come into Your kingdom." Jesus answered him, "Truly I tell you, today you will be with Me in paradise."
-- Luke 23:39-43

He looked down from the cross as He was dying, rested His gaze on the ignorant assassins and forgave them. Shortly thereafter, He looked to His left and right at two men who were deserving of the gravest consequence for their sins . . . and He forgave.

Maybe we should pay better attention to what Jesus thought was important enough to be among his last few words, delivered through the suffocation of his final breath.

One last question. Is it possible to forgive someone and for them to not really know you have? I suppose it could be, in a selfish sort of way. We could convince ourselves that we have forgiven them, but not stoop so low as to actually tell them. Perhaps that would soothe our hearts somewhat and allow us to walk away. Like the repentance and the consequences, the suffocating sinner's awareness of such forgiveness is "not my problem." I know what it feels like to walk through life without the peace of having been forgiven by some.

But why? Why give a hoarded and protected and precious gift and not allow the forgiven the possible pleasure of healing from it? Why respond to someone's longing and never let them know? Why put *their* peace beneath *your* pillow so only you can sleep at night? Maybe we should be a bit like Sampson and confuse it more with love.

Love is patient, love is kind. It does not envy, it does not boast, it is not proud. -- 1 Corinthians. 13:4

What keeps you from forgiving? Are you too impatient, too anxious to see the repentance worked out to completion and the consequences borne first? Are you biting back out of personal pain, unable to find kindness for someone who is also hurting? Are you holding back because it just doesn't seem like they deserve it, and you're not really sure you want to see them restored? Or . . . are you just too proud? Maybe they haven't asked for forgiveness and you don't want to extend it until they humble themselves enough?

Do you lack the love it takes to forgive? Ask God. In the blink of an eye He can review the span of all human history and tell you quickly that whatever has been done can be forgiven. It will cost you nothing. He already paid beyond whatever measure you might be imagine.

169

CHAPTER 32

A CONTINUOUS ODYSSEY OF GRACE

I will always be one who looks back. Out of my past, with all its levels of conjured contentedness concealed between cushions of deceit, I draw my emotion. In the losses, I find my determination. In the pain, I uncover energy to search for the truth of healing. In the regret, I discover grace. Out of the stupidity of ill-conceived actions and words, I hunger for wisdom. In the layers of the past, I see the unfolding of the future.

On some days, it is as if I am still there; on others it is as if I never was. Such is an Odyssey of Grace, a clumsy reconciling of sin and shame with healing and forgiveness, a digging out from beneath the weight of hate and sorrow into the light of love and acceptance.

Grace.

We count our years as we go through life, but completing a year makes no difference, no matter what we say or wish. One year is replaced by another. Turning a page on a calendar has about as much impact as the breeze created by the action. If we are here today and gone tomorrow; if we cannot add a single breath, then what does one day mean? Nothing . . . and everything.

It depends who holds the day. In my hands, grasped tightly and held against my chest beneath my darting and suspicious eyes, a day is a like a wadded and blank sheet of paper.

In God's hands, open and exposed to His penmanship, a day is a treasure unmatched. Its promise flows upon the page. It is good and it stands as His great invention of time. It counts. Just as He counted them in the beginning:

And God said, "Let there be light," and there was light. God saw that the light was good, and He separated the light from the darkness. God called the light "day," and the darkness He called "night." And there was evening, and there was morning -- the first day. -- Genesis 1:3

And He just kept counting them.

Day Two: He separated the waters and made the sky.

Day Three: He made land and seas and plants and trees.

Day Four: He made the stars and the sun and the moon.

Day Five: He filled the oceans and the skies with just the right creatures.

Day Six: He created a man and a woman, and He said: "It was very good."

Nighty-night. You guys sleep tight beneath that brand new moon I just made and I'll wake you in the morning with the glory of a brand new sun.

And here we are, a debatable number of new days later, on an odyssey to make the best and get the most out of however many He has ordained us. Each breath is by the grace of God.

In retrospect, glancing over our shoulders, if we have embraced grace, a year is not quite the frightful thing it appeared when it was building furiously on the horizon and bearing down upon us with its thunderous claps of "what ifs" and its threat to deliver upon us everything we so richly deserve. In retrospect, we can see, in what we thought would just be wreckage, the underpinnings of our prayers and the glorious glue of . . . grace. Somehow, despite us, the year the Lord made is there, nicked and scratched and torn and bent by our handling, but surviving still for the times we stopped, perhaps sobbing, and handed it back, like a child who too roughly played with a favorite toy.

"I'm sorry," we say. "Can it be fixed?"

And, in His way and in His time, He mends and restores and replenishes, leaving here and there a tear, a scar, to remind us of the roughness with which we treat His gift of each new day.

Grace.

Don't leave home without it.

I seem to begin each new year with these words: "I'm fine."

Fine? Despite the harsh realities of reaping. I entered each recent year still separated from my children, some past church issues still unsettled, my not-quite-completely-resolved mind stubbornly challenging my clearly-resolved soul for clarity and purpose. But I'm okay, I declare. Or, to use that all-purpose Christian four-letter word: I'm fine.

I quickly follow that up with these words: "But I'm broken."

I've come to see that anyone who struggles with sexual brokenness -- and if you think that term is too lenient and soft, just try thinking of *yourself* as "broken" -- feels as much pain about their malady as I do mine.

Men who are attracted to men and women who are attracted to women are looking for something missing within themselves. They're broken.

Men and women who are addicted to pornography and lose touch with all reality, hide their shame and their addiction behind smiles and shrugs. They're broken.

Men and women who are seeking sex with other men and women outside of marriage, whether as curious and uncontrolled singles and teenagers, or as adulterous and wandering marrieds? They're broken.

Men and women who give in to rampant self-satisfaction -- masturbation -- are losing touch with real relationships and can't explain why they find themselves more pleasurable than others. They're broken.

Men and women who abuse and control each other to show their power because they know they're weak. They're broken.

Men and women who hate and fear each other because they don't know how to love and need each other? They're broken.

From brokenness . . . to hopefulness.

For the person who struggles with sexual brokenness, life is not always nice and it is certainly not packaged for ease of opening. Nor do all the pieces seem to easily go together, if they're even all there. So we decorate the packages and overlook the missing and broken pieces and do our best to assemble the best life we can with whatever went into our basket at checkout. Sometimes it shows; sometimes it doesn't. It depends on our marketing skills and how well we sell ourselves to others . . . and to ourselves. We know "the truth is out there," but we prefer to be in here. We curl up with a little of the truth like a too-small blanket and want for greater comfort and security.

Is it "quiet hope" or "bitter resignation?" Is it waiting or wilting? When rains come, do they wash us clean and set our feet to freedom or will they be the final flood that grows ever deeper to sweep us away?

Or does the Grace of God form a dam and hold us? When do we need this grace?

When we are "fine?"
When we are broken?
When we are bitter?
When we are resigned?
When we are lonely?
When we are guilty?
When we are longing?
When we are hopeful?
Yes.
There is Grace!

Grace is not one of those great rewards extended to others who seem grace-worthy, but withheld from you or me because of the depths to which we have stubbornly clawed . . . putting ourselves in places that seem unreachable to the limited and normal grace of men. God's grace is not manufactured and manipulated and measured out. Like God . . . is . . . grace . . . is.

Grace comes upon us when we are least deserving and perhaps too fearful and ashamed to even ask. "I'm sorry. Can it be fixed?"

Grace unfolds like the tapestry of the countryside when you drive around a corner or top a hill and see in the glow of a sunset the glory of God's great creation unfolding before you and you find you are in it.

Grace unfolds like a soft yellow blanket over a peaceful sleeping child as you pull the fabric back and see the calm and hear the quiet coo. . . and an unfolding tiny fist reminds you that you really can let it all go.

Let go of what? All those things tucked deep inside the folds of your life: the tortured temptations that have rampaged and ruled, the relationships that have unraveled and ravaged, the set-aside dreams, the held-back hopes, the vanquished visions. The darkness of every day is chased away in the light of grace.

When does the next leg of this Odyssey of Grace unfold?

When we recognize we are sinful and tend to take the wrong path.

When we realize that our sinfulness is a rebellion against the very God that has cleared our path.

When we admit we know all this and resign ourselves to helplessness, that we have been lost and stumbling, ignoring our guide.

When we trust in God's willingness to forgive and again shine the light for our feet to follow.

When we actually accept that forgiveness and take His hand to lead us out of the darkness.

When we stand in the clearing and look around us at the underbrush and tangled clutter from which we have been rescued.

When we stop and look up, surrounded by threatening but held-back darkness and observe the brightness of the night sky and the sweet comfort of the approaching dawn.

When we know we are not alone.

When?

When we realize that on the day -- the sixth day -- when God made the man and the woman, He knew He would also make you. And He said: "It was very good."

Let your when be now.

CHAPTER 33

STORING UP STONES IN PLACES OF GRACE

"I don't *need* this."
"I don't *want* this."
"I *hate* this."
"What *is* this?"
"Where did *this* come from?"
"Why do I *have* this?"
"Whose *is* this?"
"*This* hurts."
"I remember *this*."
"I *didn't* ask for this."
"Where should I put . . . *this*?"
One thing is for certain: there really *is* a lot of this.
I grew up in a family that accepted transition as a stable state of being. If I begin on Texas Street -- the first house I really remember -- I can close my eyes, unfold the memory map, and wind my mind down the roads of yesterday through tiny towns and sprawling cities, spooky old houses to paper-thin-walled apartments, rolling yards and willow trees to parking lots so close the headlights almost touched our front door.

Sometimes we lived among people who cared -- like a grandmother down the hall -- or ones who just stared, like the woman in a lawn chair smoking in the dark outside the door next door. Sometimes we had stuff: matching colonial bunk beds and nightstands . . . and sometimes we had borrowed beds and crates.

We culled our things based on the size of the U-Haul and the amount still owed when it was time to move on . . . and we moved on, leaving a bit of "this" behind in alleys everywhere. Detaching was as easy as attaching.

Pity me not, for I am rich with memories far greater than the mass of stuff I might have stored up in their place. Some of the memories are painful, yes, but when sifted with the others -- like swirling together shades of paint, it is a color I can live with on the walls of my life.

Still, the splash of clashing colors here and there, left uncovered, bothers me. I have painted around them, left them on a to-do-list, waiting for a better brush perhaps, or a taller ladder to stand on, or, thought I might re-do that wall in *that* color and let *it* become me. No. Not *this* time.

We should gather up all the reckless words splattered on our walls of consciousness like rocks along a creek bank and chuck them in, listening to the plunk as they hit the water and slide to the bottom, invisible. You would think forgiveness would do that. Forgive and forget, for words will never . . . desert me. Like all those old addresses, we should leave these stone houses behind and not live there anymore, but instead, the words refuse to relinquish the view when we are panning the horizon for a new road.

We have *done* . . . they have *said*. Which will linger? The deed or the description and declaration of it? Even if it were possible to move permanently into a pattern of purity, the sting of description would cast its shadow on that land. Whether we were proclaimed by those who struggle with "lesser things" as just weak and self-serving . . . or were dismissed as an apostate beyond redemption for having succumbed to repetitive sin -- the crop of our addiction -- the words and labels affix themselves. The cruel eye-jabbing by Christians who become absorbed in the failings of others -- "You've sinned against all Christianity for all eternity," my ex-pastor told me -- pierces the heart and builds a wall the sinner never could.

If we let it.

I think one of the most difficult steps a struggler takes is learning to listen . . . and not. Listen to God. Listen to those God sends your way to speak on His behalf. Listen to the Holy Spirit

176

speaking in your stillness when you close the shutters to the outside interference. Listen to God's Word. Listen to those who have walked your path and know the pull and pain . . . but are finding victory and want to share it.

Don't listen to those old echoes that Satan whispers into your hopeful thoughts. If I allow all the things that have been said *to* me and said *about* me and predicted *of* me to swirl around in my mind, they become like a whirlpool and I am swiftly drawn under, away from God's truths to Satan's lies. It really doesn't matter whether the words were thrown our way in justified anger, reactionary pain for the hurt we caused, or just in the releasing of the air of Christian superiority from the supposed unfallen, they all pile up like stones to ground our souls from soaring, tethering us to the past.

Even when we have been dismissed by some as beyond hope . . . and find ourselves the target of their judgmental silence . . . we hang on to the words they once used in misguided motivational efforts to shock or shame us into freedom. Echoes, stored for later reverberation. Preserved syllables that slip out to form an obstacle course for hope.

Here are words to remember . . . which have hopefully been said to you:

> Jesus loves you.
> Jesus redeems.
> Jesus restores.
> Jesus forgives.
> Jesus knows.
> Jesus hears.
> Jesus wept.
> Jesus paid.
> Jesus can.
> Jesus will.
> Jesus has.
> Jesus is.

Here are words to forget . . . which may have been said to you:

Uh . . . uhh. Not here. Forget those. They may have seemed justified at the time; the shock value may have jolted you into a real desire for repentance. You may have needed to hear them then to force you out of denial, to face the falsehood and find a thirst for the truth. Maybe those words woke you up to who you were. But . . . if you are moving on, then repeating them to yourself now only takes you back to there. Don't go.

Much like taking our sins to the cross, we need to load up a bunch of hurtful words and leave them there also. Words we said, either in defense or defiance, and words launched at us like heart-seeking missiles which we pretended to dodge, but which lodged deep inside us.

Here are some words I hope you *have* heard and *will* hear from a brother or sister in Christ and that you will never forget:

"I love you."
"I forgive you."
"I am here."

Speak and act as those who are going to be judged by the law that gives freedom, because judgment without mercy will be shown to anyone who has not been merciful. Mercy triumphs over judgment! -- James 2:12-13

Mercy triumphs.

But He gives us more grace. That is why Scripture says: "God opposes the proud but shows favor to the humble." -- James 4:6

Grace is abundant.

Christians, no matter how sanctified and justified, need to "practice" mercy and grace. We don't come across these traits naturally. If we did, we would not need that still-small-voice inside us that occasionally puts a finger to our lips and hushes our natural ways so we can hear beyond ourselves and know that there are thoughts beyond our own which are better and purer, able to do more than point out faults . . . and indeed, point to promises.

Stop for just a moment and try really, really hard to believe, first of all, that God loves you beyond all your imagining and enough to have created all there is and you because of that love. Then try to think of what He wants to say to you. His voice is greater than all those others that will rush in to fill the void of silent waiting. So, wait. Do you hear Him?

That's grace . . . despite what you've done or who has spoken of it and judged you for it and believes you can never move beyond it . . . He speaks the truth to you about it . . . and about you. And about what the two of you can do.

About . . . even . . . this.

You have searched me, Lord, and You know me. You know when I sit and when I rise; You perceive my thoughts from afar. You discern my going out and my lying down; You are familiar with all my ways.
-- Psalm 139: 1-3

To God, we are not a passing thought, a momentary project. He does not move on. He knows not, "oh, well." He searches us. He is familiar with all our ways. He knows us.

Based on all of that, He always knows what to say if we will but clear the clutter that clogs our ears, and listen.

What a sweet, sweet sound.

CHAPTER 34

SILENT STATUES
IN A GRACELESS GARDEN

If I was still climbing, you'd steady the ladder.
If I were in pain, you'd ask what was the matter.
So why all the silence when you see me falling?
Why turn away slowly when you hear me calling?

If grace flows so freely, then why are we silent?
If God says to give it, then why so defiant?
If grace we've been given so we keep on livin'
Then why so be so graceless to the other forgiven?

Is my sin so mighty and I'm so to blame?
While yours is so silly it's not worth the shame?
Is that what grace does, covers sins just so small,
That we wouldn't really need grace much at all?

I truly don't think so; I think we're all wrong
If our grace is for some and not for the throng.
So why are you silent, when ladders are falling,
Reducing to whispers the cries of the calling?

'Tis grace helps the fallen to rise to his feet,
While the lack of grace lowers him down to defeat.
God's grace, we all know, is abundant and free
To choose who receives it is not up to me.

Human Beings, like plants, grow in the soil of acceptance, not in the
atmosphere of rejection -- John Powell

One of the benefits of living in apartments and duplexes most of my growing-up years was that yard-work was pretty much someone else's problem. Still, we occasionally lived in homes with fairly good-sized yards, and, being a boy, I was expected to mow. It helped that I had an older brother who was the first on-call, though he was too soon gone, his motorcycle affording a means of escape from anything that did not appeal to him, like lawn-mowing. I have to admit, my memories are more of my mother putting her full weight behind the push mower, which was always choking on the too-tall weeds that tended to mark our yards, but I did do my share.

To me, the mower was power. I would survey the yard with all the Bermuda grass "antennas" sticking up jaggedly and envision them as TV antennas over the thousands of homes that populated the yard, living rooms filled with lazy, hapless viewers . . . and then I would put myself into a spirit of annihilation and let the destruction roar and roll. "You're next," I would say to a plot of green-ville and would even, every now and then, decide who was living in the "house" I was about to shred.

I was indiscriminate. If you were anywhere between our porch and the curb, your house and all within was going down. How dare you get out of control in my yard? Nothing short of perfect 3/4" submission would be accepted. Grasshoppers and doodle-bugs that didn't flee surrendered the right to be.

I would not have made a very good God. I was into whirling blades, not unlimited grace. Yes, I know it was just a yard and it all grew back with vengeance, but in my metaphor-making machinations, I was a cruel master.

And then life continues on and the mower becomes the mowed and wonders "where's the grace" of which we all so boast? Can Christians be known for our love and, at the same time, recognized for our lack of grace?

181

I remember one day when, with company on the way and a garden that had been graced with Oklahoma's extreme weather -- 106 degree days followed by six-inch rains -- I found myself on my knees furiously pulling two-feet-high weeds from around hidden vines of cantaloupe and cucumber, their fruit mis-colored and mis-shaped by the absence of sun under the crowded shadow of choking weeds. My grown-up mind reflected on my boyhood of the antenna-crunching of the innocent, but I had adapted to the passage of years and the gain of life's experience to a better metaphor.

"You're next," I would say to a clump of weeds as my gloved hand reached down to the base just above the roots. Only this time, I found myself ripping judgment from the ground, plucking harshness, dislodging rejection, culling out complacency, digging up haughty arrogance, pulling prideful finger-pointing. I would pause and look around and realize the never-endingness, the impossible task of getting every weed. When I viewed it as a landscape, it seemed impossible indeed. But when I focused on just the weeds before me, each came up and eventually the so-craved-sun found the distorted fruits of the hidden vines and shined like grace to say it's your time again to grow.

I know what grows in the garden in the absence of grace. It is bitterness, the mis-shaped fruit of those gasping for grace, thirsting for forgiveness, reaching for restoration, but hidden beneath the weeds of rejection and crowded out by the jungle of judgment. Grace tends the garden so the root-bound can grow again.

Withholding grace from those who sin and repent. . . is a sin. Like the weeds that came into the Garden with the original fall, the weeds of withheld grace take root in the spring, choke out the summer and become the harvest of autumn.

A man or woman who struggles with a habitual or addictive sin -- such as acting out on same-sex attraction, heterosexual or homosexual lust, viewing pornography, committing adultery -- learns that these particular sins are deemed by many Christians as too slippery for the grip of grace.

Maybe the deeming is not official, but more an expression of Christian-correctness, as much as culture's approval of almost everything is deemed political-correctness. As Christians, many of us just can't handle the reality of sexual sin. Steal my bread and I'll forgive you and work out the repentance of repayment. Slip into sexual sin and I'll . . . forgive you perhaps . . . but regard your repentance as an exercise of repetitive futility. Once a pervert forever a pervert.

Okay . . . I said, "many Christians." I have found that the vast ocean of Christianity is populated with fertile islands of the forgiving who cultivate grace and hope and believe in mercy and kindness. Their lighthouses are welcome beacons to the wrecked vessels being tossed about on the seas of rejection. Grace heals and rebuilds and makes the sinful once again seaworthy.

Interestingly, these islands of grace are more often than not populated with those who have received grace themselves in abundance, people who themselves fell and looked up to find a hand extended, offering grace. Come to think of it, that should be all of us.

After years of struggling and falling and finding fewer hands extended, I understand the great pressure placed on those who offer grace "once again." As if it is in limited supply, there is a tendency to hold it back for someone more worthy. But . . . then . . . it becomes not grace at all. For no one ever will be worthy. No one deserving.

Those of us who have been shown grace by those we hurt, should be the most generous purveyors of grace. We have been given much and from us much should be expected. We even must find a way to extend grace to the ones who reject us and consider us worthless, because just as in the absence of grace, the weeds of bitterness grow in its hoarding. So, give.

Not lazy, hazy, spacey grace, but clear, powerful, unrelenting, unchallenged, full and . . . unmerited . . . grace. Stun the devil with clarity. Be self-controlled and alert.

Your enemy the devil prowls around like a roaring lion looking for
someone to devour. Resist him, standing firm in the faith, because you
know that your brothers throughout the world are undergoing the same
kind of sufferings. And the God of all grace, who called you to his eternal
glory in Christ, after you have suffered a little while, will himself restore
you and make you strong, firm and steadfast -- 1 Peter 5:8-10

The God of all . . . grace.

The withholding of grace to each other is the height of selfishness, to keep something which is unlimited away from someone who is in need. To look at ourselves and fear the embarrassment that the person we pick up may fall again and leave us with some proverbial egg on our faces. To stand back, pretending patience, when what we are really doing is passing judgment and piling on with piety. If we keep grace in a precious box because we have decided that the person to whom we should give it will just squander it and return to sin again, we are assuming the worst of both the sinner and of God. How can we in our own limitations determine when the sinner will drop the idol and claim the grace?

To the roots of the mountains I sank down; the earth beneath barred me
in forever. But You brought my life up from the pit, O Lord my
God. When my life was ebbing away, I remembered You, Lord, and my
prayer rose to You, to Your holy temple. Those who cling to worthless
idols forfeit the grace that could be theirs. But I, with a song of
thanksgiving, will sacrifice to You. What I have vowed I will make
good. Salvation comes from the Lord. – Jonah 2:6-9

Are you up to the challenge of giving grace and letting God deal with the graced and his or her sin?

Giving grace is an act of courage.

Giving grace is an act of the will.

Giving grace is an act of fearlessness.

Giving grace is an act of selflessness.

Giving grace is an act of trust.

Giving grace is an act of love.

Giving grace is an acknowledgement of the grace we ourselves have been given.

If we are but cold silent statues in a graceless garden, we have forfeited the tending to others. Blinded by our own coldness, we cannot even see what grows, we cannot turn and reach, but are frozen in our selves. Nor do we care; we are there for others to see, immobilized on our granite pedestals.

Step down. Pull some weeds. Bring grace like rain to the thirsty vines.

CHAPTER 35

THE LENGTH OF A GRACELESS DAY

I had a stepfather once named Michael who was so twisted in his own understanding of self that his greatest pleasure was found in setting others straight. He so blatantly displayed his personal demons that it made it difficult to even criticize him because he had come to the point where he was proud that he was able to function so well despite the weight of them. In a sense, his sinfulness became like a badge of honor, as if he were saying to everyone else . . . "Just imagine if I were not so burdened with all this. Why, I'd be perfect."

So he belched, walked around half-naked all the time, scratched inappropriately in front of school friends, drank himself into a stupor on occasion, wrecked cars, sold other people's personal items to get another bottle of whiskey, snored in the recliner for hours, dropped his cigarettes on the carpet, swore like an entire fleet of drunken somebodies, and complained about the mistreatment and lack of respect he received from his wife and stepchildren, who tended to tiptoe around him, preferring a sleeping big old baby to a profanity-spewing big bad bear.

I know I did not extend grace to Michael. As a child, I knew only to keep my distance and obey as much as was reasonable, not out of respect, but out of reality, realizing that as totally non-functional as he was, he was at that time our best chance to keep the electricity running. I didn't know what grace was anyway, and, while some grace may come naturally to us, most grows in time as we receive it ourselves and understand its immense value.

I remember one night at dinner when Michael, whose moods did not really mellow that much when sober, was teaching us the rules of polite society. We were learning that when you finish your meal, you don't say "Thanks, Mom. Can I go now?" No, you say, "I have eaten sufficiently. May I be excused?" Of course, for some reason, Michael had taken the word "eaten," and made a new one "et." "I have et sufficiently. May I be excused?"

It didn't matter if we had "et" sufficiently. It only mattered if we exited politely. The belching master in the terry-cloth bathrobe at the head of the table did not care if we starved, as long as we performed. "You may be excused."

Some of the most-troubled people in our lives can project the greatest pain on us, projecting their self-professed superiority with such confidence that we sometimes just accept it, realizing that to battle against it in a weakened state is futile. They may not really believe in themselves, and may actually be pretty fragile, but their very nature demands that you believe in them and accept their assessment of you as . . . gospel. The result? Infliction of rules that are not real, judgment unwarranted, insight that is beyond cloudy, a bowing to knowledge that is not there. We cower under their proclamations, accept their pronouncements, unquestionably follow their groundless requirements and stumble along, determined to please them in the hope of diminished interference. It's not altogether clear most of the time whether they mean well or actually know what they are doing, but whatever it is, "it's for your own good."

These are the ones who believe more in the gut-wrenching, in-your-face, smack-down reality of a boot-camp recognition of your horrible sinfulness than in the peace-granting, hope-building, re-constructive reality of glorious grace . . . grace which makes you grateful and aware of God's greatness. Like a hit and run driver with a more important appointment to attend, the drive-by correctors knock you to the curb, glance in the mirror just to make sure it was not a fatal blow, and speed on down the road, confident that one more sexual pervert has seen the light.

Of course, there are others whose lack of awareness runs more to the kind and gentle, a sad dismissive nature that believes everyone can be healed in the "it's all right, honey" glow of acceptance and affirmation. Here's a Kleenex; lean on me. Want to watch a little TV? You'll feel better about yourself when you've had a cookie and get some rest.

And there's the big dilemma? To clobber or to cuddle? Of both responses to my sinfulness, I have et sufficiently. May I be excused?

I wonder sometimes if we properly measure our relative "godliness." At the height of my useless defense of self when my sexual brokenness came to light, I found myself compared to "godly men," and my shortcomings -- listed sin-by-sin -- were clear. I was declared beyond a doubt *not* godly.

Is it possible though, that our distance from God's intent might be better-measured not by how sinful we are or have been, but by how graceless we have been or are? I have a feeling each takes the same measure of forgiveness, but one may actually be easier to repent of. Personally, I have seen more repentant sinners turn away from their sins than I have seen the bitter judgmental turn towards the dispensing of grace.

If you're among the sexually-broken, or just a sinner in general -- the room just got more crowded -- you need grace in a much greater proportion than grief. Maybe, the way most see it, you *deserve* the grief and you *don't deserve* the grace. That's what makes it grace.

Can you imagine a graceless day? We would be endlessly chanting in a doleful drone an alternate verse to *Home on the Range*.

Oh, give me a home where the naysayers roam
Where the angry and pointing ones prey
Where seldom is heard an encouraging word
And the skies remain cloudy all day.

A graceless day would begin with the rising sun of rejection, sending us to the empty cupboard where we were sure grace had been stocked in sufficiency. The forgiveness we hope for has fizzled in the absence of grace, yet we remain hungry, searching the storehouse for the hope of restoration, only to find it padlocked and the key misplaced. Wandering in an ever-weakening state, we would seek someone who could differentiate our person from our presumed identity and find us worthy. But on a graceless day, all these will have wandered like sheep and gone astray. There is no grace to light the path back into the fold.

Without grace, we meander, ever closer to the abyss, less willing to warn others that they too are on the brink of tripping into the graceless gray of uncertainty. Imagine, if you can, that there is no answer to all the wrong you've done and the ones who done you wrong? What if all we could do is take it like a man . . . no Son of Man having taken it for us?

No grace? Get me out of this place. Both here and there are no-where. What is the length of a graceless day? It's eternal. May as well hunker down and sit around in a bathrobe and belch.

It's hell. So far removed from the throne, it is the only place you can't find grace.

Therefore let us draw near with confidence to the throne of grace, so that we may receive mercy and find grace to help in time of need.
-- Hebrews 4:16

Feeling rejected? Draw near.
How? With confidence.
Where to? The throne.
Why? To receive.
What? Mercy.
And? Grace.
Why? To Help.
When? In time of need.

I know that in your struggles, as I did in mine, you feel sometimes like people don't care, don't know, don't understand, don't believe you *want* to change, don't believe you *can* change,

189

don't want to wait any longer, don't have any more answers; don't have much hope; don't extend grace.

For every don't of man, God unfolds a million does'es.

This is not a graceless day. This is a day that God wants you to remember that His grace is unlimited. And when you receive it, proclaim it and respond with hope for restoration and a leaving-behind of the things which shadowed it. Grace is given to who you are so you can be who He wants you to be.

In Him we have redemption through His blood, the forgiveness of sins, in accordance with the riches of God's grace that He lavished on us with all wisdom and understanding. -- Ephesians 1:7-8

Next time you struggle to make your struggle understood by those from whom you crave grace, remember that God already understands and He lavishes *His* grace on you. It's sufficient. Rise and eat sufficiently, to be excused. The morning can break through the graceless grey to become a glorious day.

CHAPTER 36

WHO REALLY NEEDS
TO COME OUT OF THE CLOSET?

I stumbled, fell and cried out but my brother shied away
And I found myself alone in silence, wishing he would stay.
He quickly turned the corner, as if he hadn't realized,
I'd turned and looked to him in pain, with pleading tear-filled
eyes.

I saw my brother stumble so I quickly looked away.
I'll ask him how he's doing on perhaps a better day.
I heard my brother crying but I quickly realized
He'd not be wanting me to see the tears that filled his eyes.

So we're just keeping distance till again it all seems right
And saying a little prayer or two before turning in at night.
No reason now to get involved, there's nothing much to say
Both blind; both fine; both better off this way.

*Carry each other's burdens, and in this way you will fulfill the law of
Christ. -- Galatians 6:2*

"Imagine, if you will," comes the Rod Serling voice, "A
church in the middle of a very ordinary town, with stained glass
windows, cushioned pews and friendly faces at the door. We've
arrived on a very ordinary Wednesday night, just in time for the

pre-prayer-service meal. Elaine sits in her usual place in the middle of a long table, in the middle of the fellowship hall . . . in the middle of it all."

"Did you hear about . . . . ?" said Elaine, her voice trailing off a bit as she lowers it, looks side-to-side, and begins to share the news with those in hearing range. Her fork is poised in the air over a plate of ham, sweet-potatoes, peas and carrots and a buttered piece of bread. Elaine is one of the best of the best when it comes to church gossip and ears quickly bend her way.

"Elaine, you're just like a dog returning to its vomit, I see," says the pastor in a calm and steady voice as he approaches her table.

Elaine stops, puts down her fork, squirms in her seat a bit, gathers her plate and purse and moves on down to another table.

"Well . . . I never!" she says. "Did you hear what he said to me? You will never believe."

Again, the voice interrupts: "Elaine, you gossip because you think it is fun, but you're just like a dog returning to its vomit."

Elaine, now in shock, sits, ponders, sets her fork gently down beside her plate and says "You're right, Pastor. I confess to the sin of gossip and I ask for your forgiveness and help in repentance."

"Sorry, Elaine," he answers. "This has gone on too long. You've confessed before and here you are, at it again. I don't think it is possible for you to ever stop gossiping. And, while I say this completely out of love for you, I think it's best for all of us if you just leave and not come back. We'll vote on it Sunday night, but basically, I think the tribe has spoken."

So Elaine puts out her torch, which means in this case, stifles her tongue, and leaves immediately. Life goes on, post-Elaine.

Obviously, this is a greatly-exaggerated account. Sin is more subtle; response more nuanced. The Elaines among us are not that blatant in their sin; the pastors not that direct in dealing with it; the church members not that silent an audience. But, in

192

real life, there is a great deal of confusion about how to deal with sin among the believers, particularly when the sin seems to have so firm a grip and especially when that sin is something that we can not easily dissect or dig down to the root cause. We see it flourish and, like a weed among the flowers, we want to pluck it out.

Of course the pastor does not intervene and Elaine is not removed. She finishes her pie and her story with a flourish, confident that her words will be repeated by others, giving her a sense of belonging she can't seem to find any other way. She keeps on top of all the latest because she needs to be needed and knows no other way. Her sin is gossip; her fear is loneliness. We should start with her fear.

Andy gets antsy about halfway through the prayer meeting, looks at his watch and yawns. The pastor noticed Andy was pretty bleary-eyed already when he came into the church, but Andy just explained that he'd been glued to his computer all afternoon, trying to get a big project done. Andy was anxious to get home and finish the project in his home office: feasting on XXX pornography over the Internet.

Like a dog returning to its vomit? Perhaps. Extending a season of fun? Maybe. More likely feeding a secret addiction that has wrapped itself so tightly around Andy that most of life has now been squeezed from him and he is bound to meaningless images and fantasies that strip him of any dignity and slowly drain from him all the sensitivity he once had toward his wife and children.

Lindsey is 17. As usual, she has worn her favorite long-sleeved turtle-neck pull-over to church and sits in a silent, pouty position at the far end of a back-of-the-room pew. She is listening in, but looking down as she rubs her arms and twists her hands, fighting back tears, but smiling weakly whenever she's approached.

"Are you okay, honey?" a sweet voice asks.

"I'm fine," she answers, mustering her familiar weak smile, her bangs hanging over her dark eyes.

"Well, of course you are, sweetheart," comes the reply. "And God loves you just the way you are."

Lindsey will cut herself in the bathroom when she gets back home, inflicting another physical scar for the pain she feels inside and can't reveal. And then she'll give her mom and dad a peck on the cheek and lay in bed wishing for sleep, longing for peace.

Terrance skipped church altogether on this Wednesday night and is walking along the trails of the city park a few blocks from his home as the sun slowly dips behind the trees. He collapses on a wooden bench and puts his head in his folded arm, looking every bit the part of a breathless runner who has pushed himself to the limit and needs to rest. He *is* at his limit. He hates himself because he is not like the other boys at his high school and he doesn't know why and he's afraid to ask himself or anyone else. The dark descends like a comfortable blanket, hiding him. He wants to cry.

"If I'm gay, I may as well just kill myself before my Dad does."

Prayers are wrapping up in the comfy sanctuary. All the pending surgeries have been covered. Missions have been blessed. Traveling mercies extended. All have confessed their weekly falling short, and everyone is ready for a little free time in front of the TV. The DVRs are getting full and need relief.

Elaine and Andy and Lindsey and Terrance are sinners, awash in their own shame, hardened by the indifference of the Christians around them, those who are to be known by their love. All four need surgery. They're all a mission. They're traveling . . . and they really need some mercy. Their lives are playing out like the scripted dramas everyone is rushing home to submerge themselves in . . . but they're real. And they're Christians . . . and God does indeed love them just as they are. But if He loves them too much to leave them there, why don't we? If he can acknowledge their sin and respond with His grace, why can't we? If He can look straight into their hearts, why are we looking over their heads?

Maybe they should come out of their closets? Elaine should just confess that she's a sad, lonely and empty woman who wants attention so badly she will spin tales for it. Andy should just come clean and tell everyone that instead of having real relationships, he slips himself into naked fantasies, in vulgar opposition to the life he models in his deacon role. Lindsey should explain that she is punishing herself at 17 because at 16 she gave her body away to a 19-year-old who said he loved all of her . . . and then left her to go love all of someone else. And Terrance? Terrance should share about his self-hatred, acknowledge the sense of rejection that triggers his misguided search for his masculine identity through improper same-sex interaction and his concerns about an eroding resistance to temptation.

Unsaved? Not Terrance. Not Lindsey . . . or Andy or Elaine. Precious ones, never alone in their sin, but accompanied by a Savior who knows Elaine could spread blessings instead of gossip, that Andy could live and love in reality, deleting the addictive fantasies that have claimed his mind, that Lindsey could forgive herself and wash away the mistakes of her past, that Terrance could see himself as God sees Him, instead of seeing himself as the broken one with no choice but to submit to the world's definitions.

Christians all, but guarding secrets in what should be the most loving and healing environment on earth, the church. These four represent so many Christians who struggle in secret with the things of this world, surrounded by people who should be safe and welcoming, known by their love, pouring out forgiveness, willing and able to hear the confessions, extending grace, offering a shoulder for comfort, a hand for support, a word of encouragement and a pledge of accountability through the walk of repentance. While he should be hearing "come on out," the sinner in the secret closet sees himself more like the spider who tiptoes through the space below the door only to find someone waiting with a broom and a dustpan on the other side.

For most sinners, the fear of what will happen if they emerge from the closet is greater than the fear of the sin locked inside there with them. In my decades-long struggle with homosexuality, habitual cover-up had a greater hold on me in some ways than did my habitual sin. The what-might-happen seemed more threatening than the what-was. I would do almost anything to keep from being discovered . . . and eventually I convinced myself that *exposure* of my sin would harm more people than the *practice* of it. Suffering through the struggle in silence was better than the risk of real-time retribution. In time, all of it -- the secrecy and the revelation resulted in an avalanche of epic proportions and seemingly uncountable victims. There was no longer enough room in my closet for all the junk I accumulated. It was spilling out the door, leaving a trail of sinful crumbs down the hall.

Maybe we should *all* come out of our closets? We who accepted the sacrifice of Jesus so we would not die in our sins. We who praise Him for His love and hoard our own, as if He could not provide an ample-enough supply for us to share with others. We who mutter "there but for the grace of God go I" and then stand by and watch others go there. We who crave mercy but are too distracted to share it. We who are so clean, washed as white as snow, startled into silence by the stains of others. Snug in our eternal life, we watch others die around us. We who walk in the light, but quench it in our closets of comfort.

Do we, for some reason, think our callousness about the ravaging toll sin takes on our brothers and sisters somehow shows us to be strong . . . because we are unwavering in our righteousness . . . and our determination to keep our hands clean?

God knows what the Elaines and the Lindseys and the Andys and the Terrances and the Thoms are going through, how they got there, and when and if they are going to get through it and beyond it. And He also already knows how He will use their struggle for His glory and to accomplish His will. Maybe they're not so happy about the journey on which He has allowed them to embark, but he knows how long the tunnel is and who can help them make it through. He also knows already whether you are going to respond or reject. He knows whether you will venture out of your safe closet to help them clean up theirs.

If "they," the observant non-believers -- whoever they are and we really should want to know -- are to know us by our love, then we may never be known. Not if we cannot bring ourselves to embrace the broken ones that Christ has placed within easy reach: the Elaines, Andys, Lindseys and Terrances that pull themselves together enough to come into this place in hope there will be more than peas and prayers.

We can only blame it on culture for so long . . . and then we need to unfold our shoulders and bear the load. We need to stop giving in, declaring hopelessness, wagging our heads with faces curved by condemning grimaces, removing the sins that might taint us by driving the bearer from our midst.

In truth, some Christians do reflect the love of God and display His grace . . . but they need some reinforcements to reach out to the ever-increasing wounded who can only be healed through the love of Christ, shared without restraint by the redeemed.

As imperfect as our church may be, sinners will not find something better beyond our walls. They do not wash away sins "out there," they celebrate them and proclaim them as identity, taking pride. If we see our brothers sinning, but dismiss even the slightest hint of a true desire to repent and fold our arms in front of us in defense instead of wrapping our arms around their shoulders, it is we who have surrendered, not they. Will it be warmer out there around the fire of distorted acceptance? Shall we just wish them "god speed," and give them no reason to even continue to believe there *is* a God . . . who lives inside *us*?

Come out of the closet. Andy's pornography addiction will not defile you when you make a plan to call him up and check on him and set up some time to get together for healthy distraction. Lindsey's past looseness will not topple you from your purity when you listen to her cry and tell her that not only does God love her, but you do too . . . and that you will stay by her side as she walks out of her past. You will not become gay by

197

standing with Terrance as he searches for the person God created him to be and walk with him through the trials and struggles of seeking wholeness. You won't lose your reputation by loving Elaine and listening to the truthful needs of her heart as she shifts to sharing blessings. Your love might be one she shares.

Jesus was a gentle savior who reached out his hands to those in pain, who knew the secrets of the strugglers and did not turn away, who stooped down to lift up, who risked his own reputation to help others build a new one. He knew how to love . . . and He told us to be like Him.

We're so often not. Maybe that's why we're in the closet.

In *His* pain, he freed us all. In *our* pain, we bind others up in theirs. Unable to share our own failings, we hide them behind our holiness and increase the intensity others feel by comparison. In the light of our inflated righteousness, their wretched sinfulness retains a greater grip on them as they strive to keep it from being seen. In the discomfort of our own cover-ups, we overcompensate in pointing at others when their covers are pulled back. We didn't want to know . . . but well . . . now that we do . . . we've go to do . . . something.

But the fruit of the Spirit is love, joy, peace, patience, kindness, goodness, faithfulness, gentleness and self-control. Against such things there is no law. -- Galatians 5:22-23

In our closets, we store the fruit -- love, joy, patience, kindness, goodness, faithfulness, gentleness, and self-control -- that would nourish the broken souls that wander around the door.

God must surely wonder how we can be so blessed and so bereft of sharing it. The abundance is unimaginable, but we bury it instead of investing it. Do we for some reason believe He can't handle all of this?

Some of us are in closets of cloistered Christianity. Others of us are in closets of condemnation. Whichever closet you are in, there is no reason to be there. Not with overflowing grace, unlimited forgiveness, boundless mercy, unfathomable love, enduring healing, eternal peace.

Please come out. Someone stands at your door and knocks.

Give Elaine something to really talk about.

CHAPTER 37

THE GIFT
THAT KEEPS ON GUILTING

Through before and through then and through forever after,
Through sighs and through tears and through too-little laughter,
Through pain and through sadness, through anger and fear,
Through wandering away and through clinging near.

Through pits of deception and mountains of truth,
Through hope and through striving, through longings of youth,
Through moments of stillness in search of Your voice,
Through dangerous journeys of self-proclaimed choice.

Through brokenness, hopelessness, running and hiding,
Through moments of peace and through blessed abiding,
Through hiding and fighting and self-disappointment,
Through moments of quiet mid healing anointment.

Through rounds of returning, through routes of remorse,
Through seasons of sinning as self runs its course,
Through rejection and judgment and waves of emotion,
Through confession, repentance and return to devotion.

Through exhaustion, bewilderment and endlessly trying,
Through pleading, demanding, blaming and crying,
Through distraction, attraction and refusing to race,
Through moments of stumbling while gasping for grace.

Through lovelessness, bitterness, through guilt and shame,
Through pointless excuses and efforts to blame,
Through uncertainty and blindness, missteps old and new,
Through Your love I have learned that You carry me through.

Few things have confused and confounded me more than guilt. I understand why we feel it and that we rarely do without deserving to, but I also understand why God designed a way beyond it, which, like so many of the great things God designed for our good, we reject and re-design, attaching words like "motivation" to it to make it sound good or "infliction" to make it sound bad. Truth is, guilt just . . . is. We shout it, tout it, internalize it, deny it, bury it, design a whole new life around it, stamp our own on our foreheads, hammer others with theirs. We motivate with it, devastate with it, testify to it, bow to it, and build a whole big room in our minds to cowtow to it.

We make examples of the guilty instead of models of the forgiven. You would think some people believe Jesus' main reason for coming was to point fingers of accusation and pin people down with their sins rather than to heal with hands of grace and free them from the very sins by which we decide they should be known. If guilt is so great and powerful, then grace is not so immeasurable after all, which, of course, is not true. We put guilt on a big-black pedestal and keep a close eye on it because we are so familiar with it, while we revere grace from afar like it is beyond our reach behind the barbed wire of the guilt-barrier we pace behind.

We need to take a clue from what God considers good and valuable. Christ died to give us grace and take away guilt. I think we're getting this one wrong and the casualties are mounting. Scriptures warning about sin are not designed to make us feel bad forever in guilt-induced holes in the ground, but to lead us to repentance so we can place our feet on higher places. You can't get there unless you leave the baggage of guilt on the barren ground where once you stood.

Does this mean that we should not feel bad when we do things we know -- or learn -- are wrong? Of course not. God gave us feelings too, which we set about to define as good, bad, hurt, inappropriate, strange, whatever. You feel bad because you're guilty. You sinned. You follow those feelings back around to confession and repentance and cut them loose . . . or, as an alternative, you can wind them around your neck really tightly until you can barely breathe. That's guilt.

If you are sexually-broken, you may have had sex with people you should not have; lusted over people God did not intend for you; used people who were not in your life for that purpose; abused your own body; cluttered your mind with images of others tangled in the messy quagmire of troubled and misplaced want and need; contributed mightily to the addictions of others . . . and lied about it all to keep yourself going in all the wrong directions while all the while you just wanted somebody to tell you how to get out before you're outed.

And then, just in case you don't feel guilty enough, someone comes alongside and says you're just doing it for the fun of it, as if self-satisfaction has not become a ravenous Venus flytrap and you no more than just a little fly, so self-diminished. You want to fly off and be all good now, but your wings are just so weak.

God also gave us memory. If you remember what it was like to strain under the weight of guilt and then to soar upon the wings of grace, you can make better choices, which He also allows. You have free will: drown or climb.

"I have the right to do anything," you say -- but not everything is beneficial. "I have the right to do anything" -- but I will not be mastered by anything. You say, "Food for the stomach and the stomach for food, and God will destroy them both." The body, however, is not meant for sexual immorality but for the Lord, and the Lord for the body. By His power God raised the Lord from the dead, and He will raise us also. Do you not know that your bodies are members of Christ himself? Shall I then take the members of Christ and unite them with a prostitute? Never! Do you not know that he who unites himself with a prostitute is one with her in body? For it is said, "The two will become one flesh." But whoever is united with the Lord is one with Him in spirit.

Flee from sexual immorality. All other sins a person commits are outside the body, but whoever sins sexually, sins against their own body. Do you not know that your bodies are temples of the Holy Spirit, who is in you,

whom you have received from God? You are not your own; you were bought at a price. Therefore honor God with your bodies.
-- 1 Corinthians 6:12-20

God's Word is clear. You do have the right to do anything, but that doesn't mean it's right to do it. In fact, there's a clear choice: Honor God. That's not guilt avoidance. It's gratefulness.

Grace calls for gratefulness.

Know God.

Honor God.

No guilt.

The next time a fellow Christian tries to encumber your pursuit of freedom with a reminder-laced boatload of guilt, producing the list of wrongs we all deny we keep, ask him or her to show you in the Bible any verse that justifies their actions or instructs them to place obstacles in your path to restoration. Remind them that putting on the full armor of God to face the world does not mean they can substitute the hammer of truth with a sledgehammer of guilt and go after others with it. Challenge them without harshness though; you don't want to inflict guilt.

We can't mix guilt and grace in a bucket to come up with a color that covers the wall and pleases all. It's a choice, like good and evil, truth and lies, love and hate, death and life, faith and doubt, sin and sanctification, lost and claimed. Choose one of each: good? love? life? faith? sanctification? found? Or . . . evil? hate? death? doubt? sin? lost?

I'm taking door number one and the bonus of grace, which opens my eyes, lifts my head, stirs my heart, moves my feet and begins to put the distance between me and the guilt and the mongers of such.

In my own life, I wish I could have been strong enough to turn away from all the entanglements I too-easily embraced. I loved my wife and my sons and my daughter and I wanted my children to love me and be proud of me and want to honor me. But, I didn't turn away; I turned life inside out. In fact, my own actions have separated my own children from the fifth commandment. (Yes, I feel guilty abut that too.) I thought somehow I could satisfy all their needs and gratify all my wants at the same time. On top of feeling guilty for all the things I did which put a distance between us, I bear the head-smack of stupidity and the impact of ignorance.

But for the grace of God. And the hope of heaven.

If you are struggling with sexual brokenness – or any habitual sin – the devil will use the mighty weapon of guilt and wield it in such a way that it casts a shadow across your searching eyes and threatens to block the light of grace. Don't give him that.

Your self tells you that you should feel really guilty about what you have done in your life, and doubly-guilty about how it has affected others. But if that guilt leads you anywhere but to the throne of grace, then you're just wandering. Satan prefers self-talk to self-control, just as he does guilt to grace. He wants to keep you mumbling in circles of mind-numbing remorse and shame.

Avoid the trap of guilt. Accept the gift of grace.

CHAPTER 38

WHAT WOULD YOU DO
IF I SANG OUT OF TUNE?

What would you do if I sang out of tune?
Would you stand up and walk out on me?
-- The Beatles

Memory is a curious thing. We all -- making an assumption here -- have things we would like to forget, to prescribe back to the unreachable nether-lands of the gray matter. Poor choices, regrettable actions, misspoken words, pain -- self-inflicted or otherwise -- times of loneliness and rejection, missed opportunities, experiments gone awry, painful partings, dumb days and blind nights.

At the same time, most of us fear the loss of memory. It's unnerving to pry open a box of "precious" mementos too long in the attic and sift through, wondering where something came from and why it was elevated to keepsake level. It's baffling to look at photos of people and wonder who they were and why you posed, clicked, developed and kept.

We don't have a very effective sifter, do we? Wouldn't it be nice if memory were like panning for gold? All the gritty sand would slide through and all that remains would be the gold and the good, the valued and treasured times. Of course . . . not only is it true that not all that glitters is gold, it's also true that not all that is gritty is bad. It's the mix of our memories that gives us both hope and wariness to keep us climbing and to remind us of the pain of falling.

When we're little, and as we grow, great attention is paid to pinning deeds to reminders:

Don't forget to brush.
Don't forget to put the seat down.
Don't forget your lunch.
Don't forget to call.
Don't forget to write.
Don't forget me.

Some of us who go through periods of separation from others in retribution for our sins -- perhaps forgiven but not forgotten or maybe neither -- may spend a bit more time sorting through the memories, finding that the gold and the grit are inseparable and oddly-balanced to bring us through to *where* we are and to make us *who* we are, as well as building a foundation on which we now build *what* we will be. It's a mixed-up matter of then and when.

Probe your emotions and you'll find your most valuable memories. I think my earliest memory of all may be of a violent thunderstorm on a summer night during a family vacation in Yellowstone National Park. The lightning turned the night sky white and the thunder shook the ground beneath the small khaki tent where I lay paralyzed ready to meet the Maker I didn't even really know about yet. I was a tiny boy in pajamas and a sleeping bag and couldn't find enough voice to scream. This then is my first real memory of fear. Suddenly, my father's frame is silhouetted against the flaps of the tent as he reaches in and then climbs in. My first memory of security.

When I was in elementary school, the teacher told us all to bring a towel to class which we would spread out on the floor to take midday naps. A ways into the school year I awoke at home one morning to find my towel had never made it from the washing machine to the clothesline to dry. I draped it over a furnace and the heat burned it brown down the middle. I begged for another towel, but instead had to take the damaged one. I spread it out on the floor and the kids laughed at me. That's my earliest memory of shame.

Love is a little harder to pin down in the memory banks because, if life is as it should be, love begins amid squeals and grunts with teary kisses on tiny feet. But who remembers all that? Oddly enough, though, it seems to me that one of my earliest memories of knowing I was loved was again on a vacation. This time in Galveston. All I remember really is that it was 1960 and my mother decided to cut our vacation short because Carla was coming. I didn't know who Carla was, much less that Carla was a hurricane. I just remember sitting on an outside patio at a Kentucky Fried Chicken, drumstick in hand, watching the clouds coming in and thinking, for some reason, that I was the most important thing in my mother's life. She must have said something -- now sifted away -- that made me feel that way. The details are gone, but the memory remains.

My first real memory of loneliness? A mixture of the day my father drove away and the day he broke his promise to return.

My first real memory of acceptance? The day a molester put his arm around my shoulder and told me I was a special boy.

My first real memory of rejection? The day a molester put his arm around another little boy's shoulder and looked me coldly in the eyes.

My first real memory of accomplishment? The day a teacher told me God had given me a gift and that I would always be a writer. (Teachers were allowed to talk like that back then.) I don't remember being told I was good at anything before that day.

My first real memory of guilt? That's a tough one. I think we work pretty hard to bury those memories, though they form a path like broken glass beneath bare feet, piercing into us whenever we try to move forward on heel and toe. I think maybe the earlier memories of guilt have been so buried beneath more recent ones that they're like splinters over which hard calluses grow. I can't always feel them, but I can see the bump.

My first real memory of helplessness? I think perhaps the ups and downs of my upbringing gave me a false sense that I would always be able to find a way out of every situation, that there would always be an answer, a solution, a repair. I would find a way and make it work. So . . . the memories of helplessness are fresher for me. The day my sexual sin of acting out on unwanted same-sex attraction was undeniably revealed . . . and

207

then again . . . and I realized only God had the answer to that. And, even more fresh? The day my children walked away . . . and stayed away . . . and I realize only God has the answer to that.

Some memories are recalled for chuckles. Like the time I took the stage with a group of guys who suffered an epidemic of stage fright, and in a collective spell of voice-tightening and lyric-forgetting, left me to solo on, an unforgettable moment everyone who was present can share in forever. The audience reaction answered the age-old question, "What would you do if I sang out of tune?"

Fear.

Security.

Shame.

Loneliness.

Love.

Acceptance.

Rejection.

Accomplishment.

Guilt.

Ahh . . . memories, not all so precious.

I think my largest cache of memories comes from searching, a jumble of being lost in total darkness on occasion and of emerging into the light on others, of falling deeper into and of struggling further out of, of trying to *find out* who I am . . . and of trying to *forget* who I am, the latter of which we cannot ever really do.

Fortunately, even though some people will pin us forever to the memories they have of us, we don't have to do that to ourselves. Even if we can't get rid of the memory of the been-theres and done-thats, the regrets and the head-scratching, we don't have to lay them out as markers to keep us on predictable paths, as if Memory Lane were a permanent address. Not all memories beckon us back. I may think some memories just should not be kept at all and I may try to bury them -- or, in more politically-correct terms -- suppress them, but instead, I just need to trust that, if they're there and can't be prayed away then they are likely there to stay, for my good. Maybe it's a good thing I have been gifted with a good memory.

One thing I will always remember are those who remembered all the good about me and did not let the revelation of the bad eclipse it. One thing I may have trouble forgetting is that so many embraced my faults so mightily that they reinvented me in their minds, measured me by my darkest deeds and walked away. According to my memory . . . none have returned. Maybe in those cases it is better to rebuild with those who have no memories of you at all.

Memories can haunt you, or they can help you. But, whatever you remember about yourself and what you have done, don't forget that God also remembers.

Remember, Lord, Your great mercy and love, for they are from of old. Do not remember the sins of my youth and my rebellious ways; according to Your love remember me, for You, Lord, are good. -- Psalm 25:6-7

Mercy . . . love . . . the goodness of God. When you are entrenched in remembering who you were, remember who He is.

For I will forgive their wickedness and will remember their sins no more. -- Hebrews 8:12

Remember the time that you sang out of tune? He did not stand up and walk out on you. Maybe we can't choose what we remember and every sin at some point comes back to wander around in our minds and hearts . . . but God *can* choose and *does* choose to remember them no more.

Don't forget . . . He is God after all.

CHAPTER 39

NOTE TO SELF: "I FORGIVE YOU"

I read about a man who "threw in the towel," so to speak. He gave up the good fight and surrendered to -- no, accepted -- as he might put it, his inner gayness . . . the "real me." He fought the fight for decades, perhaps not as well as he would have wanted to when in the midst of battle, too little pushing through and too much giving in, but clearly with the hope of overcoming. I don't doubt that, as I know you can search and cry out, even as you hide and act out. He had raised his family, served his church, built his career, and -- perhaps being generous here -- had been married for more than 25 years.

His new philosophy? My turn.

Pro-gay advocates point to experiences like his as revelation, as a celebration of a man who has embraced -- finally -- his freedom, and as proof that "no one" ever really walks out of homosexuality. They will point to the "evidence." He spent his life in church, had been thoroughly counseled, confessed and repented repeatedly, but had finally, through self-awareness, come to the realization that God made him "that way," and that fear-mongering believers had repressed him, hated him, rejected him, neglected him, even, in some odd way, perverted him. In our ever-changing please-yourself-at-all-costs society, the enlightened -- though admittedly depressed -- man makes his choice. As a Christian, he can even find a gay-affirming denomination that will provide him with a fits-all theology to soothe the pain of his past and project him into a glorious re-defined future of self-realized bliss in a community of acceptance and constant support. Never mind that such a community will never truly exist this side of heaven

I heard recently from another man who, so tired of hiding his porn-addiction, but so fearful of revealing it, has retreated into the shadows of self-satisfaction. The fear that his Christian brothers might discover his addiction has driven him to choose it over them. The real people in his life are slowly being replaced by air-brushed images. The love he cannot seem to find in the imperfect world is now provided by the perfect people of pleasure that he will never meet or ever know except in his eye-glazed fantasy life.

I've tried to think through the reality that too many Christians today are walking *away from* a life centered on Christ and *into* a lifestyle centered on satisfaction. They are seasick from being tossed about by the waves and caught in the swells between the declining churches that stand strong on truth and the growing impact of a culture that chooses its truths as if were cruising the breakfast cereal aisle, a little crunch, a bit of fiber and a bunch of sugar and preservatives. The sweet life forever. Do they walk away from the Christ-centered life because, while it worked for them in most respects, they believe it did not in regards to their sexual self-understanding? Was the easy yoke just not easy enough? The rewards pretty good, but the obedience unbearable?

It's one thing to look at what we might consider the burdens of life and say, "my turn." It's not always justified, but people do that all the time for reasons that have nothing to do with sexual identity. It's entirely another thing to look into the ever-present face of God and say, "my turn," and then walk away in search of a more suitable Savior. That has everything to do with identity . . . spiritual, relational, sexual . . . anyway you define it. Deep inside, in the truthfulness of our hearts, believers know that we cannot survive with a split identity. In other words, you cannot be "gay-identified" and "Christ-identified." One rules and the other riles against the one that rules. It's the two-master concept.

So, why do some Christians wage the war to the glorious end, comforted with the knowledge that the battle scars will fade in eternity, no matter how wearying and consuming they may be in this life? And why do some Christians, upon discovering what they have been deceived into believing is their true identity, point fingers back at the church and unload upon it the condemnation, shame and judgment they perceived -- in many cases with full justification -- that they received and internalized, even as they walked among the flock with a hidden heaviness in their hearts?

I think it is the leanness of love and the falseness of forgiveness that reflects the frailty of the church to confront the chaos of culture. We've done a miserable job of promoting the pillars of Christ's approach to sin. We've been so focused on defining sin and labeling people that we have been woefully poor at putting into practice the remedy. We would rather be a church of perfection and punishment than a church defined by love and forgiveness. We have not demonstrated that we truly believe that people can be made new, so it is not so surprising that they look for the newness somewhere else. I'm still amazed that so many in the church are anxious to know what the Bible says about the sin of homosexuality but have little interest in what Christ had to say about redemption. If we were talking in a physical realm, would you go to a doctor who told you you had an identifiable condition but who refused to write a prescription? Why then are we surprised that those among us hear from us that they have a debilitating affliction, but we offer nothing to them because we haven't really learned what to say or do?

We say want to be like Christ. Truth is, some of the people who end up -- willingly or not -- confronting their sexual conditions within the church are more likely to throw themselves into the well than to walk away with living water. Others are so damaged by the reaction to their "sin above all sins," that they are inclined to pick up the stones before the church does and pound themselves with guilt and shame.

When I became sin-identified -- known by all as that guy who did "that" and lied about it -- I found myself establishing a checklist of forgiveness. God, my wife, my kids, my pastor, my elders, my Christian brothers and sisters. God's forgiveness was assured, as He is true to His word. My wife's forgiveness was given, as she is true also to His word. Checking off the first two helped start my healing, but what of the roadblocks that remain? The other hopes on the list?

212

Sometimes we need to revise our lists -- add and subtract -- with one eye on the hope of Godly grace and the other on the reality of human shortsightedness. Christ made forgiveness look easy, because he was without sin . . . and I believe not to forgive is sinful. Regardless, it is not so easy for most people. While we should not grant them a pass on it, we should pass on beyond them and move forward in patience . . . to finish the list.

The name we tend to leave off the list, to our great detriment, is our own. To the struggler who has witnessed every single account of his own repeated failings, the mantra is often "I cannot forgive myself."

Yes, you can. And, if you are ever going to heal, you must.

Then Peter came to Jesus and asked, "Lord, how many times shall I forgive my brother or sister who sins against me? Up to seven times?" Jesus answered, "I tell you, not seven times, but seventy-seven times." -- Matthew 18:21-22

Sometimes I think this verse in the Bible where Christ provides some clarity to the question about how many times we should forgive was put there for me to understand the stamina needed to forgive myself. Yes, I know it applies to our brothers and sisters, but how many times did I look in the mirror and say "I can't?" He says, "You shall."

We have to remind ourselves that forgiveness is possible only because Christ paid an incredible price for it. When we look into our own eyes and into our hearts and in a silence in which only He and we dwell and we say "I forgive you," we know that He already has. The words cannot be hollow. They cannot be said as mere salve on a wound that we intend to pick open again. Forgiveness is meant to be healing.

We can still hope to complete our checklists. It is of great value to us that others forgive us. It would be of great value to them as well, as is everything we do that is Christ-like. It may be that they are holding it back until they think we deserve it, in which case we may never get it. Forgive them.

Sometimes we have to forgive ourselves even if others do not, or we risk joining them as stumbling blocks on the road to recovery. Can I say with certainty that the men above and others would still be "fighting the good fight" if they had been able to forgive themselves for their past succumbing? No, even with my own experience it is hard to step into another's shoes or feel another's torment or weigh his weakness. But I do know that self-forgiveness is a formidable weapon against Satan, who prefers self-hatred, a concept with which I am familiar and one for which I should not have fallen.

Note to self: I forgive you.

CHAPTER 40

WHAT THE WINDS DON'T KNOW

And when they climbed into the boat, the wind died down.
-- Matthew 14:32

"Share one of your most embarrassing moments."

I was in a circle with a bunch of strangers at a workshop and that was the icebreaker question. Hit me with a glacier, will you? I was glad the facilitator said "one of" and not "the." My mind raced as I worked to sort through a long life of potential icebreaker break-through moments. Let's see. How about the time when I got off the school bus to find my stepfather laying on the lawn in his underwear? True . . . he's the one who should have been beet red, but he already had his mid-day numb on.

Decades later that moment is not so much embarrassing as sad. I can look back now and see that he was a man who sailed off course and could navigate only towards the eventual abyss. His approach to life was a mix of "I am . . ." and "Don't you mess with me." "I" and "me" became "was" way too early perhaps for him, but much to the relief of others. So . . . sad indeed. He was clearly focused -- or as close as he ever got to it -- on the wrong "I am."

I can't remember what I shared in the group that day, (bed-wetting on a scout camp-out?) or if I took a pass and just kept sliding along on the ice, looking for a way out. I don't remember the tales of embarrassing moments others shared either, but, after all, we weren't there for therapy. I'm sure there was some uproarious ice-breaking before we got down to the business of work. I don't remember what that was either. The work.

Some things though, I don't forget. Sometimes when I am alone with my thoughts -- which is all too often -- I confront the reality of how embarrassing my sexual brokenness has been to some, especially my children. For me, it was an overwhelming burden that had me slyly maneuvering down the curvy road with a shifting load, controls set for careening. Hopefully, my four sons and my daughter will resist the opportunity to talk about it as an ice-breaker somewhere and will instead find encouragement and support from those called by God. Some things only God can heal.

Ironically, friends and family members find themselves drifting into the same void as the struggler when it comes to real help. Amateur counselors, well-meaning and not-so, wring hands and loan shoulders, which is good, but also unload ignorant advice that should have been shelved in favor of just listening. In an area where most understand little, they spring forward into this confusing tragedy like a person who stumbles on an accident and moves the broken person to a place of comfort, perhaps piercing his lung in the process. We are not all equipped to fix everything. Families have been further divided and marriages ended by silly words of others, desperate to . . . say *something*. If wisdom is absent, conjure up a platitude or two. If you are not called, don't go. If you *are* called, learn the way.

Embarrassing stepping-stones are plentiful on the path to healing. Spiritually, it can be a bit like parading down the hall of the hospital in saggy grey socks with your hair in disarray and the back of your gown flapping open for unwary audiences who don't deserve to be subjected. Eventually you settle back into the room to face the big hypodermic of truth, the long therapy of repentance and the reality that some of the more phobic will never visit . . . perhaps for the rest of your life. Sweet though, is recovering your bearings and returning to the road.

Sometimes we have to stumble, barely breathing, into the shelter from the storm. Buffeted by the winds of culture; told by the enlightened that we should accept our temptations as healthy expressions of our inner selves . . . and act on them . . . just be yourself . . . stop this backward thinking . . . and live free. After all, no one really knows you like you so you be you. In the meantime, we're to reject the truth of the Bible and sharpen our self-defense by parroting perceived inconsistencies in an attempt to throw Christians off their game. When confronted, just ask a lot of ambiguous questions about why Jesus didn't say this and that . . . and then look them in the eye and say "If you really believed the Word of God, you'd never trim your beard or mix polyester and cotton. So there. I win."

And the wind blows. Where it goes, nobody knows.

Well . . . God knows.

But God remembered Noah and all the wild animals and the livestock that were with him in the ark, and he sent a wind over the earth, and the waters receded. -- Genesis 8:1

God *remembered*. It was time for a new wind.

The men were amazed and asked, "What kind of man is this? Even the winds and the waves obey him!" -- Matthew 8:27

These are the consistencies I like. God shows over and over that He can use the wind as He wills. And, even if the wind is the wind of culture, He will.

I think people who struggle with sexual brokenness in the 21st century are in the center of a whirlwind, choking on dust, dodging debris, gasping for breath, wanting to slow down enough to focus and find a way into a gentler breeze.

The eastern winds of enlightened affirmation -- "You were made this way and it is a personal affront to all who are like you when you engage in the foolishness of denial. You cannot change, nor should you want to. Quit falling for the misleading doctrine of a bunch of people who are following a myth."

The western winds of arrogant disgust -- "God did not intend for you to be this way and you need to surrender to Him so He can change you from the evil person you are to be like us. You are an abomination and if you don't change now, you're headed for a sad life and total destruction. Get thee behind me."

217

The northern winds of blissful apathy -- "Just be happy in your brokenness. We're all broken anyway. The important thing is to be happy. I love you just the way you are, honey."

The southern winds of willful ignorance -- "It's not my thing, but who am I to judge? As long as it doesn't hurt me or force me to change what I do, I'm cool. Can't we all just get along?"

And the swirl goes on: "You're beautiful . . . you're sickening . . . you're fine . . . who cares?"

What's wrong? Are you dizzy?

But when he saw the wind, he was afraid and, beginning to sink, cried out, "Lord, save me!" -- Matthew 14:30

The most distressing thing I have discovered in this journey is the parallel roads on which some believers and most non-believers travel. For instance, when it comes to homosexuality, too many believers doubt that anyone can change and most non-believer's believe they definitely cannot. These views differ only because one carries judgment and the other affirms.

It's discouraging to see some Christians say that with God all things are possible, but, just for safety's sake, we need a bit of distance. But . . . really . . . if God changes you and all is well, we want to know, so we can celebrate with you and give God the glory. How will we know? Oh . . . we'll know. God will reveal it to us.

Like, for some reason, God would not reveal it first to the struggler crying out?

It's also discouraging to see the non-believers who find that when they have run enough times around the circle, the easy exit is to declare that God doesn't exist and therefore we are what we are because it just happened that way. I guess if you believe that all of creation just came from a mess, then none of creation is really a mess. It's all good and we feel just fine about it. Thank God there's no God to make us doubt, like Christians do.

Okay . . . that's the discouraging stuff about which many need to pray . . . or at least those in the first group, who know they have Someone to whom they *can* pray. God knows we can do better, both as strugglers and as wannabe rescuers.

So, what is encouraging?

People who seek people who seek the Lord's truth and deliver it with compassion.

The truth is, no, you cannot satisfy your outside-of-marriage sexual temptations. (Marriage being defined as one man-one-woman in a monogamous relationship for life.) And that means *all* of those temptations, including those of the teens and singles -- heterosexual and homosexual -- who want to sleep around, the good old guys who sneak porn fixes and applaud themselves for maintaining the sanctity of marriage, the men and women who secretly lust after the guys and gals walking by in the parking lot, the serial masturbator, and yes, the men and women inflicted with a same-sex attraction they did not choose . . . but must choose to resist.

Grace is sufficient for all of us. I want it . . . I accept it . . . but I need it no more than you do. There's plenty. It opens the door to confession and repentance . . . and calm.

The winds don't know the condition of the target's soul when they blow this way and that in an effort to steer or flatten, carry or blow away. So be the calm. Like Christ.

He got up, rebuked the wind and said to the waves, "Quiet! Be still!"
Then the wind died down and it was completely calm. -- Mark 4:39

> Scared? Be calm.
> Uncomfortable? Be calm.
> Uncertain? Be calm.
> Tempted? Be calm.
> Angry? Be calm.
> Hurt? Be calm.
> Embarrassed? Be calm.
> Guilty? Be calm.

He who calmed the seas can handle all of these.

Rebuking got the attention of the wind and the waves. Truth -- the words of the Savior -- prompted action. The waves could do nothing until the wind obeyed. The fear of drowning ceased.

We're not doing very well with the issue of sexual brokenness and, like sharks in the water, culture is circling the bloody mess we're making. We can do better. It's not as hard as you think to love people Christ loves as much as He loves you.

People are drowning. If all we do is rebuke and do not do so with truth, which requires much follow-up, then the overwhelming waves will wear them down instead of the calm that could have lifted them up. Take it from one who dog-paddled for far too long, but, through the grace of God, made it to shore.

ENCOURAGING WORDS OF GRACE

CONSIDER HIDING THESE VERSES IN YOUR HEART.

Jesus said, "Father, forgive them, for they do not know what they are doing." -- Luke 23:34

One of the criminals who hung there hurled insults at Him: "Aren't you the Messiah? Save Yourself and us!" But the other criminal rebuked him. "Don't you fear God," he said, "since you are under the same sentence? We are punished justly, for we are getting what our deeds deserve. But this Man has done nothing wrong."

Then he said, "Jesus, remember me when you come into Your kingdom." Jesus answered him, "Truly I tell you, today you will be with Me in paradise." -- Luke 23:39-43

Love is patient, love is kind. It does not envy, it does not boast, it is not proud. -- 1 Corinthians.13:4

And God said, "Let there be light," and there was light. God saw that the light was good, and He separated the light from the darkness. God called the light "day," and the darkness He called "night." And there was evening, and there was morning -- the first day. -- Genesis 1:3

Jesus replied, "Blessed are you, Simon son of Jonah, for this was not revealed to you by flesh and blood, but by My Father in heaven. And I tell you that you are Peter, and on this rock I will build My church, and the gates of Hades will not overcome it." -- Matthew 16:17-18

Speak and act as those who are going to be judged by the law that gives freedom, because judgment without mercy will be shown to anyone who has not been merciful. Mercy triumphs over judgment! -- James 2:12-13

But He gives us more grace. That is why Scripture says: "God opposes the proud but shows favor to the humble." -- James 4:6

You have searched me, Lord, and You know me. You know when I sit and when I rise; You perceive my thoughts from afar. You discern my going out and my lying down; You are familiar with all my ways. -- Psalm 139: 1-3

Your enemy the devil prowls around like a roaring lion looking for someone to devour. Resist him, standing firm in the faith, because you know that your brothers throughout the world are undergoing the same kind of sufferings. And the God of all grace, who called you to his eternal glory in Christ, after you have suffered a little while, will himself restore you and make you strong, firm and steadfast -- 1 Peter 5:8-10

To the roots of the mountains I sank down; the earth beneath barred me in forever. But You brought my life up from the pit, O Lord my God. When my life was ebbing away, I remembered You, Lord, and my prayer rose to You, to Your holy temple. Those who cling to worthless idols forfeit the grace that could be theirs. But I, with a song of thanksgiving, will sacrifice to You. What I have vowed I will make good. Salvation comes from the Lord. -- Jonah 2:6-9

Therefore let us draw near with confidence to the throne of grace, so that we may receive mercy and find grace to help in time of need. -- Hebrews 4:16

In Him we have redemption through His blood, the forgiveness of sins, in accordance with the riches of God's grace that He lavished on us with all wisdom and understanding. -- Ephesians 1:7-8

But the fruit of the Spirit is love, joy, peace, patience, kindness, goodness, faithfulness, gentleness and self-control. Against such things there is no law. -- Galatians 5:22-23

Flee from sexual immorality. All other sins a person commits are outside the body, but whoever sins sexually, sins against their own body. Do you not know that your bodies are temples of the Holy Spirit, who is in you, whom you have received from God? You are not your own; you were bought at a price. Therefore honor God with your bodies. -- 1 Corinthians 6:18-20

Remember, Lord, Your great mercy and love, for they are from of old. Do not remember the sins of my youth and my rebellious ways; according to Your love remember me, for You, Lord, are good. -- Psalm 25:6-7

For I will forgive their wickedness and will remember their sins no more. -- Hebrews 8:12

Then Peter came to Jesus and asked, "Lord, how many times shall I forgive my brother or sister who sins against me? Up to seven times?" Jesus answered, "I tell you, not seven times, but seventy-seven times." -- Matthew 18:21-22.

And when they climbed into the boat, the wind died down.
-- Matthew 14:32

The men were amazed and asked, "What kind of man is this? Even the winds and the waves obey him!" -- Matthew 8:27

PROLOGUE

WE CAN BEGIN AGAIN

Can any four words be more generational than "Are we there yet?" The rambunctious and rowdy Mayflower mini-Pilgrims in the 1600s . . . Laura in the wagon headed to the Little House on the Prairie . . . the littlest Israelite wandering in the wilderness . . . Tom Joad heading to California to pick grapes . . . the huddled masses yearning to breathe free . . . anyone headed to Colorado.

Sometimes the words spill forth loudly in eager anticipation. Sometimes they're whispered almost like a dying gasp.

I remember the trips between my hometown of Denton and my birthplace of Bridgeport where the crazies lived, traveling on a two-lane "highway," up and down hills with no passing lanes, around curves and into the night, me spread out in the expansive back window of an old '50s road warrior, counting the stars and asking "Are we there yet?" Threats from both parents would bring me down to just a whisper . . . but never to silence.

Once, when our five children were all still youngsters, Lisa and I took them on a trip to Dallas for an overnight stay. The next morning, we tricked them by heading out on a different highway and continuing southeast towards Galveston, where we'd scheduled a week's vacation without ever so much as giving a single one of them a clue. It ranks as one of the best surprises I ever pulled. Still, once they realized we were not on our way back to Oklahoma and the destination was revealed, it was soon a chorus of "Are we there yet?" A week later on the way home it was the same song, second verse.

Wherever "there" is, we want to be . . . and right now would be nice, thank you very much.

Those of us who struggle with any form of sexual brokenness -- like unwanted same-sex attraction, pornography or heterosexual sex addiction or other sexual problems -- tell ourselves we are on a journey. Reading this book has been part of your journey towards wholeness through holiness.

We've usually already fallen for the promise of the Star Trek experience, trying to pray for our physical and mental molecules to reorganize on some *Father Knows Best* holodeck. Of course, with a holodeck being a simulated reality in a fictional futuristic science fiction serial, it's not so hopeful. We've tried the "Beam me up, Scotty," approach and realized God has that in His hands and is keeping mum at the moment. We can't time shift; we have to live in the here and now. We want the right reality and we want it real and right now.

We're painfully "here," but we still want to be "there" -- with "there" being somewhere where "this" -- with "this" being the sexual brokenness that is impairing our lives -- is not. I'm not completely "there," and "this" is still a little bit here, sometimes, though not like "this" once was, when I was at *that* "there," instead of *this* "there." Whatsamatter? Did I slow down your reading speed?

So, how about you? How's your journey going? And who's traveling with you? Who's perched in the back window stargazing? Who's sharing the grapes? Who's alongside pulling for you as you yearn to breathe free?

I hope reading *"Who Told You You Were Naked?"* has been challenging and encouraging for you, but I know it takes more than some well-chosen and targeted words to work lasting impact on the longing soul. So, don't pause; continue seeking.

I hope you will take a few moments to send me some feedback, or to connect with me for dialogue. We really are in this together.

Feel free to write me: Thom@Bridgebackministries.com. I hope you will follow my blog: Signsofastruggleblog.com., and visit my website at Bridgebackministries.com, where you can download for free a study guide for this book. I hope you will also read *Surviving Sexual Brokenness: What Grace Can Do* for more encouragement.

Hopefully we can continue to communicate with each other. Cultural change and the acceptance and even glamorization of the homosexual lifestyle, as well as a relaxing of sexual morality as a whole, is testing the church's resolve to be relevant and right regarding the most gripping and draining problems some men and women will ever face. *No one chooses this struggle.* Those who choose to fight against it often engage in a silent battle, sorely lacking in reinforcements. Sadly . . . we usually cannot ask "Are *we* there yet," because we are traveling alone.

We should not be on this journey alone.

Then He (Jesus) said to them, "Suppose one of you has a friend, and he goes to him at midnight and says, 'Friend, lend me three loaves of bread, because a friend of mine on a journey has come to me, and I have nothing to set before him.'

"Then the one inside answers, 'Don't bother me. The door is already locked, and my children are with me in bed. I can't get up and give you anything.' I tell you, though he will not get up and give him the bread because he is his friend, yet because of the man's boldness he will get up and give him as much as he needs." -- Luke 11:5-8

Those who want to be free need to be bold, and that boldness deserves a bold response.

For those who struggle, it is vital the church come to the right conclusion based on a clear interpretation of scripture. If not, then the sin will be allowed to take an even greater toll and the church will bear responsibility. It is not time to fold the cards and yield to culture . . . nor is it time to reject a specific group of Christians, set apart by a specific sin. This problem is not greater than the God we serve.

This journey will be longer and sadder, more costly and more tiring if it continues to be the elephant in the church.

We are not there yet.

We need to get there together.

God bless,

Thom

Additional resources to help you on your journey:

Hope for Wholeness is a ground-breaking video and workbook curriculum that addresses the complex issue of homosexuality in a biblical and practical manner. Experts in counseling and biblical teaching address the issue in concise and helpful ways. The videos make it easy to study in a group setting or in your home. The program includes 17 lessons on DVDs, with a separate video of 11 testimonies of change from men and women who've walked away from homosexuality. This material can help a church or ministry easily run a support group program. Visit hopeforwholeness.com for more information.

"Must see movie about love and forgiveness. A rare find among films!" – The Dove Foundation

Reconciliation is a thought-provoking film of heartache and triumph that will inspire you to love more deeply, seek forgiveness from people you have hurt, and forgive those who have hurt you. Visit reconciliationmovie.com for more information.

Other books by Thom Hunter:

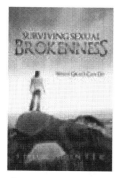 *Surviving Sexual Brokenness: What Grace Can Do* provides encouragement, hope and help through biblical truth and Christian compassion for the freedom-seeker and those who struggle alongside.

Available at Amazon.com, Barnes & Noble.com, WestBow Press, Bridgebackministries.com., and Signsofastruggleblog.com.

 With gentle humor and delightful storytelling skill, *Those Not-So-Still Small Voices* explores the joys and trials of Christian parenting through real-life tales from the front lines. Poignant, bittersweet, and often profound, these episodes will elicit chuckles from parents who have "been there," as well as provide comfort and encouragement for those just embarking on their parenting journey.

Available at Amazon.com, and Barnes & Noble.com.

Made in the USA
Lexington, KY
26 September 2013